# CANCER

## A Sentence to Live

**EVELYN REID**

**Cancer: A Sentence to Live**
Copyright © 2018 by Evelyn Reid

Library of Congress Control Number:   2017963696
ISBN-13:   Paperback:   978-1-64151-373-9
PDF:   978-1-64151-374-6
ePub:   978-1-64151-375-3
Kindle:   978-1-64151-376-0

Printed in the United States of America

LitFire
PUBLISHING

LitFire LLC
1-800-511-9787
www.litfirepublishing.com
order@litfirepublishing.com

# CONTENTS

In God We Trust

If you are asking God to do something for you like heal you, then you don't appear as if He can't. Wash you face and fix yourself up; put on your makeup: comb your hair and look as beautiful as you can. God is just beginning to show you that you can trust Him in any situation.

So have your pity party, but don't stay there too long. You've got work to do; it's your time to shine and give God the glory for what He is about to do in your life. Journal your experiences and tell others so we can take the fear out of what Cancer can do to us and show the world that God is bigger than Cancer.

Enjoy,

Evelyn Reid

# FOREWORD

# BY DONALD M. REID

All of us have had cancer!! Shocked!

Well, it's true. You and I have had cancer. The difference is that our immune systems were strong enough to fight it off. The numbers of cancer victims are growing at an alarming rate. Sometimes conventional medications are not enough to fight off this deadly disease. If you are looking for some hope that may help you in your battle with cancer, this book is for you.

Evelyn Reid fought off two bouts with Cancer, at the same time, while rejecting chemotherapy. When doctors gave her little hope, she began studying and using natural and homeopathic medicine. Along with her faith in God, the ultimate healer, she had been able to survive with a great quality of life.

Evelyn's original prognosis back in 1995 was she would be dead in five years. She is still alive! She does many of the things she has always done.

What I am saying is maybe her story will help you. It has really helped me. For you see, I've been married to her for twenty-seven years.

May God use this book to encourage you!

Sincerely,

Rev., Dr. Donald M. Reid

# DEDICATION

This work is dedicated to God my father and my Lord and Savior Jesus Christ, who spared my life and allowed me to live. To my wonderful husband, Dr. Donald M. Reid, who takes good care of me, builds me up and encourages me to pursue my dreams. Thank you love for being there for me you are truly my Sunshine!

To my lovely and sweet daughter Leni Shontae Wilson, who listens, smiles and let me share my dreams with her. She helps where she is needed and lends her shoulder and arms when I need a good cry. God gave me one of His best in you. Thank you so much.

To Beverly Wimberley, who came to my home every day and took the time to nurse me back to good health. Thank you Beverly you are truly my friend.

To my father the late Dana B. Pettie, whose words, "what can you change by worrying?" became a way of life, a figure of speech and a source of strength for me? Thanks Dad, you are beautiful to me. To my sisters and brothers, Barbara, Ramona, Vina, Dorothy, Mary, Dana Jr., Joseph B. Douglas L and the Pettie Clan without your prayers and support I couldn't have survived this ordeal. You are mighty prayer warriors and I love you all.

To my in-laws, J. W Reid, Christine Harper, Audrey, Eric, Valeiger, Kennon, Willie, Robert, David, Elvis, Arvilla and Barbara. Thanks to all of you family and friends for being there and lending a helping hand.

Finally, thank you Alethela Baptist Church Family.

*In Loving Memory of Heaven's Best*

My Mother: Martha Ruth Walker Pettie

My Brother: Patrick O'Neal Pettie

My Sister: Monica Shaneal Moyer

Sister-in-Law Earnestine Pettie

My Niece: Treketa Nicole Nibblett

*Special Thanks To:*

George Foster, Anna Loggins and Phyllis Bowman

Who worked tirelessly to read, correct and help me in this endeavor! To Rev. Louis Fortune, who encouraged me to write my findings in this book, along with the Members of The First Baptist Church of Marshall Heights of Washington, D.C., Pastor: Dr. Lehman D. Bates and The Church Family of Ebenezer Baptist Church of Charlottesville, Virginia, Pastor Lehman Bates Jr., who were the first to read my work? And the Global Faith Alliance, St. Kitts Missions Crew.

Words cannot express how much I appreciate your loyal support and help.

Thank you so much!

Evelyn Reid

# INTRODUCTION

How to Minimize the Risk of Cancer

The best way to deal with cancer is to never get it in the first place. Cancer is serious, and the cost of getting well may cause many families an unplanned financial burden. The best way to stay healthy is to learn very early how to eat to live, and live to eat well.

Cancer, how frightful is the word! Why so many people are terrified when the diagnosis comes back as positive? At the mention of the word cancer, most people go into a state of shock and immediately start down a road of depression. While at the same time, we start looking for some answers that will fix our problem and get us back into the swing of life. When diagnosed with cancer, cost and distance of travel becomes a small drop in the bucket as you focus on getting better. All we want, is to be healed, therefore. we are willing to follow any kind of regiment or plan that may prolong our lives.

Out of panic, fear and desperation, many people overload their body system with too much unnecessary worry, pain and hardship. Cancer is not always a death sentence and it does not mean that we will be sick for the rest of our days. What it is showing us is this that we should learn and teach more about our cancer, no matter what kind of cancer it is. It is now time to evaluate what is going on in our bodies and look at cancer as a way the body is letting us know that something is wrong and we need to pay careful attention to what is going on.

Cancer should be looked at from this vantage point. You are a victim. But now, you are victim in control of the task at hand. The more you know about cancer, and build on your wealth of information, the more empowered you will become. In your hands you hold an arsenal of healing knowledge. This knowledge holds the power of life and death in your hands and can last a lifetime. Knowledge is powerful. The more knowledge you have, the more powerful you will be and the better the healing and health care will be.

You, however, must first take control of your own destiny. You can make choices and decisions about your health that will give you complete satisfaction about your health and give you peace of mind.

The first step is to minimize the risk of cancer for you, your family and your community; do your homework and research your environment. Just by looking at the environment you live in, you can know what percent of the people in your community have or has had cancer. What kinds of cancers happen most often there? You must make and keep a list of the various types of cancers occurring most often in your community and your personal surroundings. Also, list the reasons and causes of death and why some people live and others die with the same diagnoses. You can even bring it closer to your home by investigating what is going on in your own personal life, the lives of your family members, and why Cancer is more prevalent in your own household.

The second step is to investigate the water supply in your area. You can do this by having the water authority in your area test samples of your drinking water and get others in your community like your neighbors, relatives and friends who live in other areas of the city/county to have their water tested also. This will give you and people of the community a better understanding of the water they are drinking.

The third step is to have your home and workplace checked for asbestos, lead, carbon monoxide, mold and mildew. You may want to check for any other thing that could cause breathing and/or health problems. Knowing facts like these will help you in your investigation of the root cause of cancer in your area.

Investigating the types of industries in your hometown can also be of great help. For example, notice if you are living and an environment that is a farming community and is producing fruits and vegetables These are things you should look at in your investigation. Take a look at the various types of chemicals and pesticides used to produce a larger amount of crops. Take notes and list the number of persons with cancer. Make certain you also note the various and different kinds of cancers such as lung, breast, uterine, colon, cervix, etc. Look at the people who remained in the environment and those who moved to another location or city. Check to see what the difference of cancer rates among the people who left and the ones who stayed. Make notes if there are major differences or changes in their health. In my case, I came from a city where a factory would release different colors of die into the river daily.

If you came from a meat producing environment, look at the types of antibodies and the kinds of feed treatments that are given to the cows, chickens, pigs or any kind of animals that are produced for the supermarkets and the stores. By getting this knowledge and gathering this data, you will help yourself and your community explores options for making decisions affecting their roads of illness and recovery. The more knowledge you have, the more you can get involved in your cure for cancer and you personally have a say in how you want to be treated medically.

In order to defeat cancer, we must know where it got its start in our bodies in the first place. This is why knowing your environment is so important. It is also important to know what kinds of foods you are eating. Knowing the food you are eating can help you determine what you should eliminate from your diet and what you need to add to your diet in order to improve your health.

Sugar feeds cancer and you should be aware of your sugar intake, at the same time you should watch out for the amount of starches in eat in a meal. In my own personal research, I have found that diabetes follows and/or Cancer follows diabetes.

It is my hope, that as you read through this information, you will gain a desire for getting involved with your own healing by increasing what you know and by doing your homework and following what you have learned. Knowledge is powerful. You can know how to help yourself and live a better quality of life by putting into practice some of the knowledge you have picked up along the way.

It is my prayer that many of you will be successful in your quest for truth and healing.


May God Bless You

Evelyn M. Reid

# THE REASON FOR THIS BOOK

I wrote this book to give people with cancer hope and encouragement to fight, to live and face life well with real joy and optimism. My prayer is for these persons to open their eyes to the vast wealth of information waiting for them to discover, and put into practice this information that can and will give them hope and a good quality of life.

When my story began, I was a happy, healthy and new Bride. I was enjoying my life and being married to my wonderful husband whom I love dearly. We had been married 5 years when we got the news about my cancer. We were shocked, heartbroken and confused. How could this happen? What could we do?

My thoughts caused me the pain of uncertainty. What was I dealing with; it was a personal battle going on in my mind. Thinking that I didn't have much time to live, and afraid of dying, I was a nervous wreck. Believing that I was saved, yet I wasn't really sure that I was understanding my salvation, in my mind I was in deep trouble.

I needed a word from the Lord. So I started by talking to the Lord, praying and writing down the deep and trouble feelings going on in my mind and heart. Telling God of the confusion and irritations going on inside of me as I cried out to Him, "Oh Lord, You made me, you know me. You know how to heal me, if it is Your will."

My first quest was to seek His face. I asked God to let me know beyond a shadow of a doubt that I was saved. I wanted assurance of my salvation. I asked the Lord to heal me and give me more time. I asked for forgiveness of my sins and the sins that I had not confessed or had forgotten I had done from my earliest remembrance. I asked him to search my heart and to reveal to me any wickedness found in me, if I had malice or any bitterness or any ungodly condition in me. I didn't want to carry with me to heaven if I were to die.

In my repentance, I stayed in His Word. His word gave me comfort and allowed me to know that my salvation was certain. Learning and knowing this took away a lot of fear and helped to lead me in a direction that would begin my quest for knowledge, and that knowledge has kept me alive and given me a good quality of life for twenty-one and a half years of survival. Thank you Lord!

When I was first diagnosed, I didn't want to tell a soul, I was just going to quietly die and not breathe a word about my condition to anyone. But, thank God for my pastor husband who said, "I have not served God all these year to not call upon Him now. We will go to the church and have the church call a prayer meeting for you." I obeyed. We called for a special prayer meeting with our church family. My church family went into prayer, supported us and showered us with an abundance of love and care.

My husband taught me from the Scriptures, what God's word told us to do when we are sick. In the book of James it tells us that when a believer gets sick, the one who is sick should call for the elders of the church and let them pray and anoint them with oil and the sick shall be healed because the prayer of the righteous availed much." Since that time, I have called on the church whenever I get sick. Now I tell everyone, "Do not go into surgery or deal with any critical diagnosis without calling on God's people for prayer. You can bank on the Word of God and believe what the Scriptures say." The Scriptures that my husband gave to me that day are found in the book of James 5:13-16.

"Is any among you afflicted? Let him pray. Is any merry? Let him sing Psalms. Is any sick among you? Let him call for the elders of the church; and let them pray over him, anointing him with oil in the name of the Lord; and the prayer of the faithful shall save the sick, and the Lord shall raise him up; and if he has committed sins, they shall be forgiven him. Confess your faults one to another, and pray one for another, that you may be healed. The effectual fervent prayers of a righteous man availeth much."

So my first step was to *"get right with God!"* After I got the peace I needed from God, I began asking Him to show me and to lead me in a direction that would help me get my mind and my body healthy again.

After my surgery, four weeks later, I was sent to an Oncologist. The oncologist wanted me to have both radiation and chemotherapy. I was uncomfortable and confused as to what to do and I didn't have peace in my mind. I needed help to make this critical decision. So, I asked God, and in my search I found a scripture that said, "God is not the author of confusion." And that was enough for me.

I went back to the oncologist and asked him to give me some statistic; I wanted some reports of how many people with my kind of cancer who had taken the Chemotherapy Treatments had survived. I waited for several days while he searched. When He came back to me with his findings and I was shocked, when he showed to me that he had only found one report. And without hesitation I said, that is not enough. He became angry with me then he said "if you don't take the chemotherapy you are going to die." At that point. I turned my face to the wall and said, "You are not God and only God can determine my death day!" At this point I chose not to take chemotherapy, and went against the advice of my doctor.

I did however take radiation and I have regretted that decision many days. Now as I look back and knowing what I have learned, I probably would not have taken the radiation either because of the damage it has done to my bladder. I never thought that after all these many years I would be still researching and seeking ways as to how to get rid of some of the damage that taking that radiation has cost me.

After my decision to not take chemo I was now free to do my own research and get involved with my own cures for cancer and look to the Lord to show me the way.

I am not telling you that I am a doctor nor am I acting like one. I am just sharing with you my story and what I did to get to this point of living with cancer. I want to make those of you with cancer aware of knowledge that is out there so you too can benefit in your quest for healing. What you are seeing here, and what I am sharing with you is some of the little knowledge and research that I have found has helped me to survive 21 years of cancer. I hope that my little knowledge will stir up a desire in you, so you too will find out as much information as you can. I know that you can win your battle with cancer as you start to investigate your own personal research that will improve your condition, help you to live a longer, have a productive life and survive cancer.

I did a lot of research and I read everything that I could get my hands on that related to cancer. Because of my quest, I was busy, reading, listening, searching the internet and getting pamphlets and books, looking up natural products and finding out how they worked, not just with my kind of cancer but on all cancers. Because of my research, I was able to come up with some simple formulas that I could afford and was able to use them daily. As you take this journey with me, I hope that some of my personal formulas will benefit you also. Of course, check with your health care provider first.

# PART I

# A LITTLE TALK WITH JESUS

Trust in the Lord with all your heart and lean

not to your own understanding.

Proverbs 3:5

*(Two and a half years after my first cancer)*

Good Morning Jesus,

Today, I just wanted to talk to you about what I am feeling inside. I did not sleep very well last night because in the back of my mine I was thinking about your decrees that I am learning about in a bible class at my church.

I know nothing is happening to me that you did not decree before setting the foundations of the world. I know that I should not be so selfish in my thoughts and desires. I even know I cannot change what you have planned for my life, but I do need to talk to you about it.

You see, yesterday a lady came into my little flower shop to sell me an ad for a church brochure. As we talked she begins to tell me about some of her concerns about her own health problems. Of course, I shared with her that I was a Cancer Survivor and had been for the past two and a half years. As our conversation progress and got deeper, she turned the conversation from her health problems and started asking me about mine.

At that point, she began to tell me about a friend of hers who just happen to have the same kind of cancer as I. She told me how she had survived for about two and a half years and how about five months later the cancer returned and she died. Before our conversation was over, she told me about a total of seven people she knew with cancer and how they all died. By this time I was very depressed. Finally, the conversation was over and she left my store, but not without taking with her all of my hope of being a survivor and living long. She robbed me of any joy that I may have had for still being alive. She made me feel like I couldn't live another day, nor could I find any reason to rejoice in the fact that you allowed me to live and to be back into the swing of life with my condition.

So, Lord that is why I wanted/needed to talk to you about this situation. It seemed so very strange to me that people can't feel what we cancer survivors are feeling or why they can't understand what we are going through as we battle this terrible terminal disease. No one asks for cancer and no one really wants to die from cancer and everyone wants a cure.

The reason I am coming to You Lord is to express to you what I am feeling because you are the only one who really knows me. You hear me and you understand the turmoil going on inside my heart and mind. I am confused and I need your help.

One of the problems that I am having is this, when a person who is not sick encounter a person like me, who is already struggling with a deadly sickness or a disease. That healthy well person has no idea as to how to handle a conversation with the sick. They think that they are helping yet with their tongues they rob that person of hope, peace and joy they may be having while they are coping with this bad situation.

Because of my encounter with this woman, whom I believe meant well, I feel a strong, urgent need to teach people how to encounter a sick person and how to stay clear of advice they don't understand. They need to be mindful of not only the condition of the cancer patient but also the family members and friends who may not be coping so well with the unknown. Until the day where there is a cure for cancer, people who visit the sick need some kind of bedside ethics. They need training on how to approach people and their families who may be at a breaking point. Sometimes family members have a hard time dealing with the diagnosis of cancer and they may need attention and answers that may be hard for them to accept at this serious but critical situation.

Cancer or any killer disease is ugly and the thoughts of having cancer can be devastating for the sick person, their families, the church family, and the workplace family. Just dealing with the possibility of cancer returning is always there in the back of their minds and the minds or those who love the cancer person. So as you can see, Dear Lord, I needed to share with you and anyone else who will listen to what I am feeling.

Hear me please, Oh Lord

## How to Talk to a Cancer Survivor

In the book of James, chapter one, James tells us to, "Count it all joy when you fall into various trials, knowing this, that the testing of your faith worked patience. But let patience have its perfect work that you may be perfect lacking nothing." And "if, you lack wisdom, asks God who give to all men/women liberally and upbraided not."

My first reaction to this young woman brought about depression and sorrow immediately. I started feeling sorrow for myself and I could not function. I spent the rest of the day crying and thinking why I should bother to live. Because at this point. I couldn't see how I could live long enough to accomplish any or the desires of my heart or finished any of the projects that I had my mind set to do. How she rob me of my hope.

Didn't that woman know she was upsetting me, didn't she feel my inner thoughts? Couldn't she see that she was causing all of my hope to disappear? My first thoughts were "oh Lord, I'm not ready to die! I want to live, I want to do things and be productive, and I want the opportunity to buy our dream a house and a chance to decorate it and I want to put my touch in it. But now because of this woman all my hope is gone."

By now, I am really depressed and I have thoughts of my dying. I also have to take my depression and this extra added burden home to my husband and the rest of my family members. I can never share with my family members just what I am feeling mainly because trying to protect them from this unnecessary pain brought on by this woman's advice. This is not a burden my family didn't need nor is it good for me to try to pretend that I am ok when she just ruined my day.

Now I'm looking for comfort and it's amazing where I found it. I found comfort in God's word!

### *Count It All Joy:*

Lord forgive me, I have allowed small things to take my eyes off you even for a second. When I take my eyes off you I discover that I can see myself quickly starting to drift away. The strange part is this, when I am drifting I feel like what the Scripture say about the ship without a sail. I feel like I am lost at sea with no anchor to sustain me at the dock or keep me stable. Thank you Lord, for it is in you I am stable and In You I am secure. Forgive me for allowing Satan to steal my joy, as I have allowed this young lady to rob me. I should have responded as a believer like one born of the family of God, yet I allowed this situation to rob me of the proper way to address her concerns. May you Lord use this situation to help me teach myself and others a way to share their thoughts, feelings and concerns with a cancer patient? Please guide me Lord as I seek to find a healthy and proper way to help people learn and know what to say or not say to those who will come in contact with a victim of cancer.

### *Here is what I found:*

Today I am not dead. I am still alive and I can still move, breathe and I still have my being. Thank you Lord, for all you do to remind me of Your decrees that all things are rendered certain about me. In your divine plan before the world begin. Nothing can happen that you don't already know.

Even though I feel depressed, I am saved. This means that if I die, I will immediately go into the presence of the Lord. Thank you. Lord for showing me how I must depend on you. And thank you, for reminding me that my hope is in you alone. It is in you and not in what people tell me. Your word tells me that "To die is gain."

I have another opportunity today! Thank You Lord for how you remind me to put the things of yesterday behind me and press towards the mark of, "A higher calling." That means, for me to not dwell on my past. so, let yesterday die. Today is a new day with glorious new opportunities.

I have family, Thank You Lord for reminding me there are those who love me. even in my condition and that no matter what I am experiencing. I am not alone. When I hurt, my family hurts, and when I feel joy, they feel joy.

Therefore, I should always remember, "You are my refuge and my strength, a very present help in the time of trouble."

## How to Communicate With a Person with Cancer:

Many people, who encounter a cancer survivor, really don't know how to talk to them or what kind of responses to give a person with cancer.

The first thing to know is that cancer can affect anyone. The more you know about cancer the better you can talk to a family or a friend who is a cancer patient without robbing them of their self-esteem and joy.

### *What Is Cancer?*

**(My Opinion)**

Cancer is a bad runaway cell in the body that has become weak and dysfunctional. This runaway cell has broken away from the rest of the good cells.

This reminds me of Satan. The story goes that before Satan fell from heaven he attracted and teamed up with a large group of demons to form a coup to take over heaven. One third of the angels fell with him. Well, too me, cancer acts in a similar way. A tumor is formed by a group of bad and weak cells. They then join themselves to each other; this is where the weak cells attach themselves together with the bad cells to form a hard mass which becomes cancer. If nothing is done, like surgery, radiation or chemo. Then this mass made up of the runaways starts the process of moving to take over the body. It can be aggressive and dangerous.

Your body however has a built in immune system. The immune system is made up of many healthy cells which go into action to protect the body from sickness and of any type of foreign matter in the body. When the immune system is healthy it takes on a warlike fight to ward off the bad runaway cells that can clump together to form a hard mass. If the immune system is not successful in protecting itself, the clump of cells then takes action by moving to another location in the body. If this cycle is not stopped, the cancer now has the ability to spread throughout the body to a variety of locations. When this happens, the cancer eventually takes over the body and if not treated, it may cause death.

Now that you know what I think of cancer, you don't have to assume that cancer victims are sinners. And you don't have to make that person feel like they have done some disgraceful thing that may have caused cancer in the first place. It is my opinion that cancer is a definite breakdown of the immune system. Anyone, regardless of race, class, gender age or sexual orientation can get cancer.

This is why I wanted to give you some helpful information that will help you get your immune system up to par and working at its best to keep you healthy.

So, as for you healthy people and those who are curious about a cancer patient, here is a little helpful advice that will help you consider before visiting a Cancer Patient. This is a do's and don'ts list. You may want to read and reread it before going to visit a cancer patient.

# The Do Not Do List:

## What Every Person Should Know Before Visiting a Cancer Patient:

1. Don't try to find out if the person has a hidden sin that might have caused cancer. Do your research and speak intelligently and with compassion with that person.

2. Don't tell them how many people have died that you know who have had cancer.

3. Don't assume that all people have the same kind of cancer.

4. Don't tell them horror stories of death.

5. If they gain or lose weight, don't continue to harp on their weight problems. (Most likely it's the medication they are taking and they will return to normal after they are well).

6. If they lose their hair, don't embarrassed them or ask them about their wigs.

7. If you complement a survivor, let it be genuine and not an attempt to find out where their wigs were purchased.

8. Don't make medical suggestions based on someone else's diagnosis or recommendations that have not been proven to be safe.

9. Don't pretend that they will not die or that the cancer will not return. Who made you God and how do you know for sure?

10. Don't stop them from sharing their feelings about cancer, death and their fears. It is a natural process that needs to happen and you are the blessed one when the cancer victim confides in you.

11. Don't tell them to *"Name it and claim it"* for their healing, it may not be God's will to heal them.

12. Don't tell them they are not exercising faith. How do you know?

13. Don't tell them not to say the word cancer because the devil will hear them and make it come true.

14. Don't give them false hope. Let them face reality. Life and death is in God's hands only.

15. Don't tell them that the doctor isn't God. They know that already.

16. Don't ask them where the cancer is. Let them tell you when they are comfortable to talk about it and if and when they want you to know. Give them some element of privacy. They will share their story when they are ready.

17. Don't ask them gory details about their cancer, causing them to explain and re-live every little fact. Give them the right to share their story when they are ready.

18. Don't stop them from preparing for death, mentally, physically, spiritually and emotionally. They may have a need to tell someone who they are and only when they are ready. Sometimes by our own attitudes and our personal pain, we force sick people to suffer in complete silent pain and in isolation a because of our own selfishness and denial.

19. Don't try to hide cancer from loved ones, such as husbands, parents, children, in-laws, etc. Family members can be helpful in showing love, praying and giving of themselves; they too have to deal with their own pain and emotions.

20. When a family member is sick and there is more than one sibling, no one family member should assume that you have to carry this burden all by yourself? Seek out the others and be willing to let them share in this trying time. Everybody has feelings and everybody wants to do their part. Get out of the way and let all share in this process. It is a time for healing and not dumping on the others what you have done. Whatever you do, let the Glory of the Lord keep you and let others praise you. Nobody wants to hear that you did it all, now is not the time for sibling war.

21. Don't take away their authority, don't start throwing away their stuff and taking away their rights. They are not dead and in many cases they can make good and important decisions concerning themselves and their families.

22. Don't stop a conversation about someone who has cancer when a person with cancer or a cancer survivor enters the room. They still have normal concerns and can pray for that family.

23. Don't hide the death of a person who has died from cancer, from a cancer survivor, cancer is not a death sentence for all who have the disease besides they need to live in the real world, face reality, and not be in denial.

24. Don't assume that you know what that persons wished are. Ask them and let them tell you.

25. Don't try to stop a person from writing a will or an obituary.

26. Don't blame the person for what is happing to them as if they have control of their destiny.

*How to Share With a Cancer Survivor:*

1. Pray with them and for them often.

2. Send them encouraging messages of hope

3. Find and give them information that is positive and offers hope.

4. Visit them frequently. Keep your visits short and sweet.

5. Find out what their needs are and what you can help do.

6. Let the patient talk. Listen! They may need to share their fears, their hurts and their eternal state.

7. Let them talk about death if they wish. Death is a fact of life.

8. Let them plan for their children and family. It is their given right and it helps them with the coping process.

9. Let them get their proper rest, it is necessary for healing. Don't wake them if they are sleeping and don't bring friends or young active children into the room of the sick.

10. Don't make them answer a bunch of questions simply because you are curious.

11. If the sick is a member of a church family, don't everybody go at the same time and sit around having a good time at the expense of that person. Too many people bring different kind of germs into a room. Wait until the person is ready for visitations and gifts.

12. Find out before coming to the hospital what that person can have like flowers, food or goodies. What you bring may be against their medications and what their doctor's plans are for them.

13. If they are asleep when you come to visit, don't wake them. Leave a note that you were there.

And by the way if you can think of any other thing that may not be proper etiquette or a behavior that may be unbecoming when you visit with a cancer patient please govern yourself accordingly.

## This Is The Day The Lord Has Made:

Good Morning Jesus:

It's me again; it's another day you have made. I will rejoice and be exceedingly glad, mainly, because of Your Faithfulness. It never ceases to amaze me how faithful you are with us. Each morning, you give us another, opportunity to live and do something great with our lives.

Maybe I have taken the life you have given me for granted, in that I never thought of your goodness and your faithfulness or how much you cared for me, even before having cancer. Maybe, I just took life for granted, probably because I thought I would live forever or at least to the ripe old age of 92 or above in my right mind and in good health. Aging, death and dying was not a part of my agenda. I wanted to be a star.

No one could have prepared me for this disease. No one could have told me that I was going to have cancer in my life time. You see, I was healthy, or so I thought I was. My doctors never gave me any indication that I was sick. And even the little sickness that I had, I never paid any attention to what it might be. So, I went on with my life still doing the same old abuse to my body. Working hard, on the go, never resting and not paying attention to my body or the warning signs it was giving me. I was too busy, looking for my next opportunity to make it big. I did not see myself as one of defeat or sickness.

If you are reading this hook, it may be a good time to slow down. Ask God to show you what His plans are for your life and pay attention to the warning signs that may be helpful for your future. Life is short, now is the time to live.

As human beings Lord, we do not pay much attention to any of the warning signs that our bodies tells us. We just think a headache is a headache and we never find out what is causing this headache. We pop in a few pills to ease the pain and go on with our daily routines as if our problems are solved.

Thank You Lord for creating within our bodies a built in computer that is our brain that processes information that lets us know something is out of control in our body. Our brains lets us know that something is happing to our body by allowing pain to be a warning sign this pain should not be ignored. We should not pop pills just to soothe what is ailing us but only when we know for sure what the pain is and where it is coming from.

Thank You Lord for giving us a brain! It is a magnificent warning device to let us know when a foreign substance has invaded our bodies. Oh how great you are to warn us when our bodies are being attacked by some foreign invasion. Lord please let us pay close attention to this little temple in which we dwell.

My doctor told **me** that if **my** body hadn't stayed persistent with the pain I was having, I would probably be dead, because my previous test reports did not give any indication that cancer was lurking in my body. **He** told me that he would have never looked for cancer in me because by all indications 1 appeared to be healthy.

Thank You Lord for the pain in **my** case, because without it I would not be alive. The question is, when did cancer enter my body and why didn't I notice it at first **signs?** The reason is probably because cancer is a silent killer. When a cell goes bad it does not sound a trumpet or tell us what's happening. They just start a war within our bodies. Before we know it, we are being attacked and we are in full blown cancer. To me, this is the case with any disease such as diabetes, lupus, heart disease, kidney disease, arthritis, aids or any other disease that is having havoc on our bodies.

The truth is I wasn't paying attention. I was so busy doing my own thing that when my body started giving off warning signs I just ignored them and started to diagnosed **my** own case without knowledge. **By** the way, I had warning signs. I just overlooked them and went for over-the-counter medications, in hopes that my pain and discomfort would go away. The pain did not go away. It would cease temporarily, but the medicines would never completely heal me, they just put me on hold for a while. What they gave me was a false since of being healed.

Lord, forgive me for how I have abused my body, this temple You gave me to dwell in, forgive me that I did not **pay** attention to my body or take better care of it. When I look back, I can clearly see my own destruction, my own attempts to make myself feel better and my neglect to investigate what was causing my **pain** and where it was coming from. Lord, you gave me the warning signs but I fail to see them and fail to take heed.

I should have known something was wrong when earlier in the year; I became extremely tried and exhausted. Without knowledge, I diagnosed my case as having low blood, and again medicated myself by taking over-the-counter Iron and Vitamins. I thought a few days rest would solve my problems and I closed my case without any medical advice.

At that time, some of my homemade cures were only temporary bandages. They gave me a little temporary relief and again I went back to work fullforce when suddenly and without warning another sign was there. This time it was totally different, I thought I was having a heart attack. So once again, after self diagnosing myself I decided that I was having a bad case of stomach gas. So I went to work to work on my own over-the-counter medicines. Getting some relief it stopped for a few days and then returned with vengeances with unbearable pains. It was then that! knew I needed the care of a medical doctor, so I went to Urgent Care a local medical center. Because of my symptoms, they hooked me up with a heart specialist and they gave me medications that relieved my symptoms. It was at this point, I started not to follow through with the heart specialist but my pain returned and I kept my appointment.

The heart doctor ran all kind of tests on me and found our that my heart was healthy. He gave me some more medications and asked me if I were under any kind of stress. Of course, I said no. The medications once again relieved my ailing body and he sent me home. Once again, I went back to my normal busy schedule without making any changes. Relieved that I was not having a heart attack, so back to work I went, before my body was rested and ready.

Lord, forgive me for the abuse that I have put on my body by not being still long enough to let you speak to me through the warning signs you gave me concerning my health. If it is your will Lord, let me now be a testimony to others that they may never have to come to this point of sickness, where there is no turning back. Let my light shine before men/women so that they can see how powerful and wonderful you are, to give us understanding of how our bodies work. Because of our lack of knowledge and our busy intentions, cumbered by our overloaded schedules, this is what actually causes us to lose our focus about our health which in the long run, causes us much pain and suffering. As I look back, and know what I know now, it just doesn't make good sense to me now not to pay attention to what is going on around us and not be aware of what is happening in our bodies?

Thank you Lord, as I now look back. I can see things that I did not see before. My focus is different today and now I have time to see your glorious works. I now slow down to see the birds, and hear the crunch of leaves, or watch the little squirrels and they find acorns and watch them paying with each other with exciting vigor with their friends, running, jumping and living free. Your word has told us that you are a God who sees a little tiny sparrow falls, yet to you Lord, I am more than the sparrow. You oh Lord, have given me intellect, but I have failed you by not paying attention to the things around me. You have given me wisdom, but I have failed you by not seeking it with all of my heart. You have given me love, but I have failed you by being so busy with the cares of this world, that I have not seen how much you have loved me.

Lord, you have been merciful and have spared my life. You have given me the opportunity to tell others how to be wise with the body loaned to them. Lord, forgive me please! Dear Lord, please let all who read my story become completely aware of this temple, their body that they not take for granted what you have given us in knowledge. Let them hold their bodies in the highest esteem and take good care of them. Let them know that we are fearfully and wonderfully made and that we can live a healthy and productive life if we pay attention to what our bodies are telling us.

# PART 2

# DEVOTIONAL MOMENTS

# Morning Watch Devotional Moments

Thinking of You lord

Lord, lead me in your righteousness as I go along my way today. Let my heart be filled with love and compassion for your people as you have shown love for me. Protect my heart, guard my mind, and allow your servant to be equipped with your armor of strength.

Let your word be the strength of my life and my conversations. Help me to be mindful of these who will come into my presence today. If by chance, you send an angel my way, let me treat him as if you just walked into my path. Make me aware of those who have authority over me especially my husband and friend and the one who watches over my soul. Never let me forget that you are God and you alone rule the universe. Let me find kindness even for those who hate me and kind words for those who do evil things against me.

Forgive me for all my petty ways. Give me strength to overcome my little irritations that hinder me from being all that You want me to be. Help me to keep silent when I think I want to speak. Help me to listen and be attentive to someone who may need me to hear them. You know that listening is a real problem for me and I run my mouth too much. Please bridle my tongue, so that when I do speak, I will only speak what you have laid on my heart.

Help me to bring joy to a hurting heart and strength to someone who is weak. May I never do anything to embarrass you or Your Kingdom? May your peace dwell in my heart today?

*Evelyn*

Lord, thank you for the little things, such as allowing me to clean my kitchen tonight. So many times when I was very sick and unable to do my housework someone else was doing my housework for me which made me feel helpless and a teeny-weenie bit jealous. I don't know why I felt this way, because my house was cleaner than I could ever have cleaned it even on a good day.

Forgive me for my shortcomings and help me to always remember how you send us a ram in the bush, especially when we need some tender love and care. It is sometimes hard to let others love us. However, I thank You Lord for having those special people in our lives that fill in the gaps for us when we are down.

Thank you for small things we take for granted each day. Like taking a bath, hot running water and showers that let the warmth of the water flow over us and refresh us. So many days during my illness, I couldn't bathe myself but you made a way for me and had a ram there for me. Thank you for Beverly Wimberley who cared for me so lovingly while I was ill and at my worse point. Her kindness and never ending energy gave me the opportunity to relax rest and not worry during my Illness. Thank you Lord for giving us what we need when we need it. Thank you for Beverly. I will cherish your friendship and love for all eternity. Words can never express how much I love you and appreciate you.

Life is so special and filled with so many small blessing. We would never recognized them if you Lord didn't give us a chance to stop, laid down and have time to pay attention to the tiny details of everyday life. Every life has some kind of trouble or disappoint but most people don't find the small unnoticed miracles that happen to us every day.

Dear God, You are good and you are more than words can express. Thank you so much for Your Son Jesus, who came to free me, you died for me and laid down your life for the sin of the world. He came to redeem us from a burning hell. You are so awesome, more than what my words could explain. You are more than what my heart could express. Without a doubt in my heart, you are God and there is no god besides you. You alone deserve my praise.

I love you Lord.

You, Dear Lord are in my thoughts today. October 28, 2002.

Today is a new day that the Lord has given me to be faithful. Yet, every day when I allow my mind, heart and soul to wonder, I find that I am not so faithful after all. Sometimes I allow little distractions such as a phone call, where I listen to someone on the other end gossiping or complaining about something or someone else in the Body of Christ. This behavior causes me to drift away by saying something that I may regret a few moments right after I have said it.

Today as I examined myself, I wonder why so many Christians are so full of envy and strife against one another. Those who do complain usually work in the body of Christ and they complain regularly about the ones who are not working, and vice versa. They are always finding fault in what's getting done and what's not getting done or they are complaining that they could have done a better job. But my question is, "why don't you do or not do what you are complaining about?"

When I would do well, I find myself like Eve always looking for something to fill up my day. I want to listen, touch and taste things that I know might not be good for me. I want to take over areas that are off limits to me, especially when I think what I want is not getting done as fast as I think it should be. No wonder God told women that our desires would be to our husbands and he would rule over us. What I think God was telling us is this, our desire would be to move into our husband's lane and take over his position. I guess that's why women get into more trouble with our mouths, ears and eyes than with anything else. Things like the telephone, the malls, and weight tell it all. We listen, touch, and taste which makes us more like Eve than we realize. What we must do is to keep our minds saturated with God's Word so will not sin against God.

*Prayer:*

Lord please let me to be mindful of how I let a telephone conversation get me in trouble with you. Keep my tongue from evil and my mind stayed on you. Give me love and courage to tell the person on the line that I am not interested in hearing their complaints about those in the body of Christ. Lord, help me not to feel joy in those who try to engage me in murmuring against another sister or brother in Christ. Grant me the words that are seasoned with salt and the ability to teach others in a loving way in the hope of bringing that person to repentance so Your Word will not he blasphemed. Give me your peace and let me impart it to the person on the telephone line.

Thank You for this day.

November 5, 2002

Lord, its morning and so many times I have failed you by not being watchful. I get up and get so busy stirring around the house. The telephone rings and my day have already starting like a whirlwind. Again, I have forgotten my morning watch with you.

I know that my days are better when I take the time to consider You, Your goodness, your mercy, your awesomeness, your faithfulness and your Sovereignty. Even though I know this and I am aware of who you are. I still let time slip away without seeking your honor and your glory. I realize you look for me each day just as you looked for Adam and Eve in the garden each morning.

Forgive me for my careless way of thinking that I can do anything without you. For without You I cannot move, breathe or have my being. Help me to be mindful and considerate of who you are. Lord, let me revere you because you are God and besides you there is no other.

In You Lord I am everything.

I Love You Lord.

*Evelyn*

Learning is something we should never stop doing. Every day I learn something new about myself and others. Every day that I don't consult with the Lord I find that I cannot contain all of what the day has to offer me. Having to depend on anyone except God is very difficult. Lord, I hate depending on man because I need independence in so many areas of my life, yet I need to depend on you for my being.

What causes us to want to be free to do our own thing? We want freedom, yet we want to dependence too. It's like that in relationships, such as parenting, everyday communications and in the work place. We want the freedom to choose, yet we crave the approval of someone else who will approve of what we do or say, how we say it, how we dress and so on.

Lord, please forgive me and help me so that I don't stray too far from the ways I think and know I need to go. Sometimes I want to fly. Sometimes, I want to cuddle and purr and stay close to those I love.

What's with me today? I need you to calm my restlessness and give me peace when life disturbs me. You are the only one who really knows me and really watches over me and has a concern for me when I go through a day like this one.

Help me to remain faithful, seek your truth, and stay in your word. I love you Lord.

You are good to me!

Thank You.

*Evelyn*

Thanks Lord, for friends who listen and allow us to vent our frustrations. Life is full of little foxes and thorns and so many waves like that of the sea. This wave causes us to waver and if I didn't know that you were with me I couldn't survive.

Today Lord is a good day to spend time with you. Help me to be content and at total peace with you, the one who made me and forgive me when I want to go beyond my limitations. Today I feel like flying. I love to fly and soar on the wings of my mind even though I am still here in one place. I feel like a butterfly locked away in a cocoon trying hard to free myself, to talk to myself and to find peace to know who I am and what You want me to do with this life that You have given me to live in.

I need to hear from you.

*Evelyn*

Today is a good day to look for the return of the Lord. Today as I read the book of Mark Chapter 13. I realized that the return of the Lord is closer than we realized. We as Christians must be on the alert and look for Him daily because time is winding down. We must witness to those who don't know Jesus Christ.

Lord, please grant your people the opportunity to search for you today. Give your people a chance to lead a lost soul to Your Kingdom. Let your glory be a light unto our paths and allow your glory to shine through my life today.

I am so blessed to have a desire to know you. You are the saving grace of my life and my story. When I feel down, you always have a ram in the bush for me. You always have people who enter my life and soothe me with words of comfort.

Lord, you are the one who see about me and my well being, even when I am distressed and don't know that I need seeing about. Help me to be strong like a tower that won't fall. Let me be loving, kind, and at peace with my fellowman.

Thank you for allowing me to live my life in your creation and choosing me before the foundation of the world to be your servant. Let me serve you as if you are coming today. Help me to put my life in order so that at your return from heaven I will not be ashamed.

Oh God I am so glad that you came into my life. It was through your word that has allowed me to know you more intimately. You are truly awesome! You truly have the world in control.

I only need to trust you whole-heartily.

*Evelyn*

Life is full of little irritations and hardships. That's what our minds want us to think. Seems like the devil and his demons enjoy making us squirm at their tactics. They want to make us uncomfortable and unglued by the little things that come our way.

Thank You God that we have a Savior who can come to our rescue when we call for help. He is there at any given moment. He sees us and rescues us from all hurt, harm and danger.

"We have not because we ask not, and when we ask we ask in vain" We are so busy asking for stuff that we fail to get the real blessing that God has for us because of our greed.

Lord please forgive me and give me only the portions you have for me today. Help me to be satisfied with the provisions you have for me. Let me be blessed with and share of what you have blessed me with. Let me not be selfish and hording of what I have. Let me be loving and giving being cheerfully in my giving. Grant me peace and knowledge in my search for you.

My greatest desire is to know you well before I die.

*Evelyn*

Another day, another discovery! Life is full of little discoveries each day. Today I am thankful for the ability to breathe. When we cannot breathe we are in big trouble.

Thank You Lord for my lungs and I know that with each breath you are breathing for me and for this I am grateful. Forgive me for thinking I can do this without you. How unlearned we are when we try to do anything without you.

You are so patient with our ignorance. Especially, when we think that we are, "all that and a bag of chips!"

As I watch my body deal with Lung Cancer, I realize that I am fearfully and wonderfully made. You could have let me die immediately, but you spared me and allowed me to live on, so that I could get some things in my life straight. Now when I do die, I won't have to carry a hunch of garbage with me when I enter Your Kingdom.

I'm just thinking of how much mess we have in our lives. We are so small in our way of thinking as if what we think is the best way. In our arrogance we rarely consult with you God about what your views are or about what's on our minds. We just take off with our heads in the air like we know it all. The truth is, without God and His Holy Spirit within us, we are dead wrong in our opinions. I know what some may say, "God gave me this mind and I can use it any way I choose"! However, the "real meal deal" is, "is God pleased with the way you are using your mind today?"

Because many of us make decisions without consulting God, we don't realize that one bad decision can mess you up for life. Think about this. You are in a fight, you are mad enough to kill; you pick up a gun and pull the trigger without thinking. Your anger got the best of you and now, you are sentence to life in prison for murder. Why are you here? Because you didn't take the time to ask God!

Lord, help us not to move without consulting you even when we are outraged, enraged, upset or out of control. Help us to be mindful of you always and please give us peace in those moments of madness and distress. And help us make it a habit of asking you, "What's next? Thank you for making us aware of your presence in our daily lives for we know that it is only in you that we can truly live moment, minute and hour is by your grace and mercy.

It is so amazing! When I think about it, you are always there in our lives, second by second. That's a blessing! I love You Lord, because you have us covered in all our ways. You cover our coming, our going, our ups and downs and all that is within us. Thank You for creating me, but mostly for knowing every fiber, cell and innermost parts of my being. Truly there is no place I can go where you are not there. I thank you for all that.

My prayer today is for you to know me and for me to know you Lord, I thank you.

I love you.

*Evelyn*

Lord who am I that you are mindful of the things that concern me today? It's wonderful knowing that I have a God who is concerned about my every move. How awesome you are Lord. You have made the world and all that is in it. Thank You for allowing me to be a part of your creation. Thank You that you let me live in this time zone. Thank You that you have given me the opportunities to know you, to read about you and to take a daily walk with you. You are wonderful, amazing, marvelous, and awesome. You are a mighty God, the only true and living God who cares about a little piece of clay like me.

Thank you for this day. It is another day to breathe your air. How wonderful air is. On yesterday, at church I had a breathing attack with my lungs. Since I've had lung cancer, breathing has been difficult for me a times. When I got outside and into your fresh air, what a difference it made in my breathing. Suddenly, I could breathe. How thankful I am for your air and how you allowed me the opportunity to use it. Praise you Lord, for knowing what we needed when you created the world. You put every small detail mankind would need here on earth. You're a brilliant and I thank you that you allowed me to know how all knowing you are. You are not only my God and my Savior you are my friend. I hope that I am a friend of yours too.

Help me today be your witness. Fill me with your spirit and mind and let my speech and my being be full of you and bring glory to your name.

May your peace fill my heart? Let everyday you allow me to live on the earth be overflowing with your love and peace. Lord, let those who see me and know me, know that I have been with you today.

Be with me today Lord.

*Evelyn*

How beautiful it is to know you Lord. Just being a part of your world is a grand opportunity. We get to do some of the thing we like just because you have given us freedom of choice. I am so thankful to be an American where I have the freedom of choice. And even though I don't always make the right choices, I still have that right. I am so thankful to you God that you let me be born as an American Woman, and not born in the bondage of men like the women of counties like Afghanistan where the women are enslaved by their husbands in this male dominated population.

On yesterday as I was listening to Marling Maddox's radio broadcast, I was shocked to know that Muslim men in Afghanistan and that region do not believe that women have a place in heaven. They believe that if they are martyred they will go to heaven and get ten (10) virgins upon entrance into heaven where they will enjoy the blessing of Allah. How sad they are and how great our God is.

I thank you Lord that man does not have a heaven or a hell to put us in or take us out of Thank you! Lord, for creating men who know you, men who understand that the family was established by you, and men who understand their roles as heads and leaders of the family. Thank you for men who recognize that women were created by God and given a place beside their husbands. Thank you! Lord, for giving the women in our culture husbands that they can submit themselves to. Thank you Lord for men who can honor and nurture their women so these women can bask in her husband's love. Thank you for our husband's whose protection and loving eyes that can see our needs and take care of them, so we do not have to worry about any small thing that comes our way.

Thank you Lord for making me a woman and allowing me the opportunity to serve you Lord under the leadership of a husband. How awesome you are to have planned it this way. If we the people would just follow you, our lives would be so much better. Lord. I respect your plan of creation and your wisdom and divine plan for me.

Grant me the ability and health to really know what your plans are in my life and once knowing this; let me fulfill ever jot and tittle of what you have for me.

Love you much.

*Evelyn*

What's happening in our world? When we turn on the television it's all about gossip. Seems like our world we know here in America is all about gossip. We want to be informed about what's going on in someone else's life and we forget to get involved with our own.

A few days ago at a beauty school, I was listening to some of the girls talk about the soap operas. I was shocked at how many women and men were intertwine with what was happening on the televisions shows and how involved there were. They all had likes and dislikes about certain characters and they all had great opinions on how the outcome of a situation should play out. As I pondered over what they were saying, I thought to myself how sad it is that so much energy is being wasted on someone else's life, like that of a soap opera star.

They didn't seem to mind much that the soaps operas put no money in their own pockets, yet they spend most of their days blinded by what is going on in a favorite character's life. They had anger and frustration by a charter's lack of or an abundance of something. To hear them talk, one would have thought that they were talking about a real event that was currently taking place. Yet. when the show is over, the soap opera characters go home to their families, with a pay check and their families have plenty of money to live the good life.

So many women and men waste a good portion of their days keeping up with the soaps. They forget to take care of the needs of their own homes;

trying to imitate or be like a character they see on television. They are hooked, just like being on drugs and they don't know how to quit.

An actor/actress plays a role and, hopefully, has a life. People who get involved in the soaps fail to make that connection and their own homes go lacking because so much time is wasted; viewing the fictional problems of others. Many women who watch a lot of television have little or no time for their own personal appearance? The way they look when their husbands left home is the same way they look when he returns home from work and in some cases no bath and still in the same night gown they were wearing when he left.

Where are our minds? Are we so easily led astray and involved in the lives of others until we fail to live our own life?

Sometimes when my husband and I visit the hospitals to pray for someone's loved one, who may be dying, the family members and the patient's are so involved in the television until they forget to turn it down or off when the pastor come to pray for them.

My question is this. How can I hear from heaven when I allow so many distractions to blind me and cloud my mind?

As I see it, it is time for us to examine ourselves by asking if my life is so consumed with what's going on around me that I couldn't hear from heaven even if heaven was on the main line. How tragic it is too lose a loved one, but it is more tragic to lose a love one to hell. Just because we were too busy to stop, look and listen to what the Father was telling us because television had our attention.

Lord let me to have no other God before you.

Cast Your Cares on Him for He Cares For You:

Good morning Jesus, here I am again, bringing you all of my cares, for you care for me. It's great to be alive today and still be able to take care of some of the task that you have give me to do today.

However, today I just want to thank you because in your divine decrees you have given me two wonderful and great blessings. A husband who loves me and a daughter. who loves, adores and respects me How blessed I am to have these two wonderful people in my life.

Life is short, just like a vapor, just what you said it would be. Oh how quickly that vapor fades. Seems like only yesterday that I was asking you to let me live long enough to see my daughter through high school, but in your faithfulness you have allowed and granted me the opportunity to see her finish college and get a masters degree. What a blessing this has been for me? Now I'm getting greedy, because now, I want even more. I want to see her married and with children and maybe to see her children grow up and get grown. It seems as though we are never satisfied, we are constantly asking for more.

Forgive me Lord for not being content with what you have already blessed me with. For not taking the time to count the daily blessing sing you have already given me. Sometimes I see the world through rose colored glasses and I never take the time I have needed to count the cost of what I am asking you.

Am I sounding like a person who is going through cancer? I hope not, because even though I am still going through my ups and downs. I am fully aware of how blessed I am. I am really privileged to have had the opportunity to live through cancer and survive while here on earth especially when so many others can't say the same thing.

Thank You Lord for everything you do for me.

## *God's Plan:*

"I know the plans that I have for you declare the Lord, plans for welfare and not for calamity to give you a future and a hope. Then you will call upon me and come and pray to me. I will listen to you. And you will seek me and find me, when you search for me with all your heart." Jeremiah 29:11-13

Who is like our God! And who really knows what his plans are for our lives. Who knows what tomorrow will bring or even how our minds will work when we are faced with any situation that takes us out of our comfort level.

I am glad that God made us this way so we can learn how to trust Him with all our hearts, mind and soul. It seems like only yesterday that I was walking around making plans for my future and behold within a few seconds, my whole world was turned upside down, with the words of my doctor. "You've got Lung Cancer."

How could this be? I've known about the nodules in my Lungs for a year and a half. My other doctor said they were probably fatty tissues and not to worry. He said that he would watch them closely to see if any changes were taking place. In December 2001, he informed me that my lungs were O.K. He was confident the nodules had not changed since his discovery. Now it's August and the Mayo Clinic Surgeon is telling me and showing me from a CAT scan that it is cancer. How should I react? What can I do?

Every life has many stories and ever story has a life. The question is which life story is worth telling someone else about. My life has been filled with many tragedies and many sorrows, much heartache and many disappointments as well as many happy times and brief moments of pleasure.

Looking back in hindsight, God has delivered me from them all. Who is like our God, mindful of all the small print in our lives? Who is concerned for every major and minor detail of our being? Romans 8:28 says, "He has called us according to His purpose" not our own.

If we all look back over our lives it will make us wonder how we made it through some of our adventures. We will be so surprised shocked by some of our outcomes. Remember that car accident that didn't leave a scratch on you or the boat accident and we lived without drowning and to tell it. We were wanderers and ended up living in a town where we knew no one, but now look at us, we are known in our neighborhoods and we are an active part of the community. Who is the mastermind of who we are? The Bible says, "Before the foundations of the world, the Lord knew us and he predestined our lives."

Which means that in eternity past he knew me: He knows me in eternity present, which is now, and He will know me in eternity future, this is good news for me. The book of Ecclesiastics chapter 3 is correct when it says "to everything there is a season" however, between birth and death our lives are filled with many seasons. The question to me now is what season of my life do I want to tell you about?

Life is filled with many distresses and confusions. Sometimes we are afraid and hurt. We need to talk to someone who will understand the pain and the frustrations we are going through. Our frustration may come in many disguises like financial or sickness, our children, our marriages or our jobs. Because of all the trouble in our lives, now may be a good time to be still, to be quiet and talk to the Lord and stop striving. Let your hands down and listen intently, with open ears for the plans God has for you. Remember, that he is God and he has your best in mind with a plan that is suitable for you.

So many times when we are troubled, we need to talk to someone who will just take the time to listen. We don't care about their character, their views, or what their moral values are; we just want to be heard. Sometimes to our harm, we will side with people of a like mind. We like to listen to people who will tickle our ears but not give us what we need, but what we want to hear. Their words sway us in a direction that we may not take if we had been prayed-up, worded-up and filled-up with the spirit of God. It is easy to take advice when we are not equipped to handle our own situations, because we have not prepared ourselves in God's word. We rely on the knowledge of others, especially the ungodly, who always seem to be close around us, instead of relying on the knowledge of God or his people.

When we are experiencing turmoil in our lives, we usually run for cover, we will talk to anybody who will listen to our woes. We don't want to consult God or his word, we are headstrong and hardheaded. Before some of us trust God we usually try to work it out or try to fix our trouble. We seek worldly wisdom first and as a last resort, we "look to the hills for which comes our help and our help comes from the Lord."

Lord, please forgive us for looking everywhere else for answers before looking to you. I love you Lord for you kindness, even in times like these when my life is overtaxed, overburden, and overstressed. It is still good to know that is your will that none should be lost. This included even me Lord, Yes, even me.

*Evelyn*

Life is like a moving sidewalk. It is slowly moving, but not going anywhere fast in our minds. Our worlds are impacted with what's going on around us. Fear has gripped on every side. Television has consumed us and filled our lives with so much mess. The internet has taken up much of our valuable time, and our jobs and other interests have made our lives a mess.

We seldom have time to communicate with each other because our lives are all about us-about our jobs, our homes, our values, our cars, our hair, our clothes, our children, and everything else in our lives. We spend most of our time keeping up with the Jones by worrying about that others think of us. Despite all of frantic efforts, we may be failures. We may feel we failed our husband/wives our children and our neighbors, friends, community, state, parents and anyone else who might be a part of our existence.

We prepare for many things in our lives. We spend much time preparing for this or preparing for that, but I wonder how many of us are really prepared to meet the Lord? We say we are going to heaven and we see heaven as a wonderful place and this is good. But, now I wonder if we are going to heaven to be the Bride of Christ and if we are how many are really prepared?

A bride never meets the bridegroom without being prepared. We make our outward appearance attractive and perfect for his eyes, we are clean beautiful and fresh. Everything about us must he perfect and everything pertaining to our wedding plans must be in tip-top shape.

Yet, when we say we want to go to heaven to become the Bride of Christ, we want to go without really knowing the Christ whom we say we love. We have not communicated with him. We have not spent any time with him, allowing ourselves to really get to know him. So how can we say we are really in love with a Savior you don't know? I think we may be in love with heaven and what we think heaven stands for, without looking at what heaven is and represents. All they we know is that heaven has many mansions there for them and that's what most of us are hoping for. The question is, "how can we be happy in a place where the glory of the Lord dwells, and be there with a bridegroom that we don't intimately know"? Why do you want to be a Bride of Christ?

*My Prayer:*

Lord, help me dress myself as the Bride of Christ. Adorn me with your grace and mercy, and help me to be all that you would want in a Bride. Let my life shine before you as a bright morning star and please pick me, let me be like the Rose of Sharon and the Lilly of the Valley in your heavenly garden. Lord, I want to go back with you when you come for your Bride.

*Evelyn*

# PART 3

# GETTING HEALTHY

## *A Personal Manifesto*

A good number of people I meet and who know about my cancer often ask me, "How can I stay healthy and live longer?" The truth is, no one can stop the day of your death and keep you alive when it's your time to go. It is appointed once that a man/woman should die. You cannot live past the boundaries that have been set for your life by God. The day of death is in the hands of God. Therefore, no conventional medicine, natural medicine, lying on of hands or prayer can take the place of God or change his decision for your dying day.

Today, there is a lot of sickness among us and is not enough information to keep us healthy. No one has all the answers we need, to stay healthy! We are busy people, caught up in the everyday hustle of life. We have too little time to care for our bodies. In order to be healthy, our minds and body needs rest, relaxation, and exercise. These are usually the last things on our agendas! Our bodies are usually overworked, overweight, and under a lot of stress. The sad thing about this is most of us are not conscious about what is going on inside of our bodies until sickness had come in to live and taken over.

Did you know that you can play big part in the quality of life you have here on earth. Life is full of twists and turns and sickness can creep upon you at any unexpected time. One day you are well and full of life, but the next day you are sick and don't know how you got there. Sickness didn't just happen. Just like anything else, it took years of neglect and abuse to get your body to the point you got sick. In other words, it took years of not paying attention to the little warning signs, little nagging pains, little stresses, and the continual abuse of your body to catch up with you and eventually take its toll. You are not taking care of your temple that is your body that God has loaned you while you are here on the earth. And we are all guilty of neglecting and not paying attention to what God has imbedded in us through our immune systems and brains to let us know something is not right with how we are feeling. Are you listening to your body?

The bodies we have do not belong to us, they belong to God. How you treat your body is very important to God. God created our bodies for us to live in, to enjoy, to move and breathe and to have our being. He gave them to us to take care of and to treat them properly. If the truth be known and after careful review we find that most people don't like what God has given us to keep our bodies healthy. What we do is this; we add stuff that is not good for us. We try to change what nature intended to be good for us. We like to add junk to re-make the things that God said was good. We have to add our own version to nature which could be things like, sugar, flower, coloring, yeast and other artificial stuff that may be causing harm to our bodies. We don't even question the additives or what they are. We trust man rather than God. I believe that God had a purpose for everything in His creation because he said so when he placed Adam and Eve in the Garden of Eden. When we add junk to our daily intake as mention above we leave our bodies weak and unhealthy and especially when we over indulge in what we are eating. For example, we don't like to drink plain water in its natural state. We like to doctor it up to suit our tastes buds, however water was made by God and was given to us for a number of uses to enhance our living. Water was given to us for drinking, cooking, bathing, and swimming and many other useful needs and reasons to help us sustain our lives and help us maintain our wellbeing.

Some people don't like certain fruit and vegetables so they reject foods that are made by God that are good for taking care of the body. Sometimes it is learned behavior and a lot of times people just don't like what God has made for us to eat, enjoy and live healthy.

As I read the story of creation in Genesis 1:11-12 then God said, "let the earth sprout vegetation; plants yielding seeds and fruit trees on the earth bearing fruit after their kind with seed in them and it was so. The earth brought forth vegetation, plants yielding seed after their kind, and trees bearing fruit with seed in them, after their kind; and God saw that it was good." Everything God made was good and good for us. I believe that in creation, God made provisions for us to sustain life and stay healthy during our stay on the earth.

It was in the Garden of Eden that God planted a garden and then placed the man and his wife in it. Notice how he placed water in the garden possibly for drinking, bathing, and swimming and/or any other things for man and woman to sustain life. He also created four rivers to run from the garden possibly for man to enjoy and explore his creation. God made the garden such a beautiful place where man and his wife could live, work, and behold his glory.

Just like Adam and Eve who lived in the garden, who did not take advantage of all the good that God had provided for them, so too are we. We too have tried altering everything God has made for our benefits and pleasure. We have not asked any questions as to why God made what he made and what benefits it will be for our overall health. We seldom question why God didn't let everything grow all at once and why he allowed certain foods to grow in different season and what benefits the foods for that season has on the health of our body.

This is one of the reasons I wanted to write these helpful tips. So you my readers, would know not only how your bodies works but also, how the seasons in which foods were created to be eaten can play a major factor as to why it is necessary to pay attention so we can know the benefits these herbs, vegetables and fruit play in keeping you healthy. These helpful hints are all so written so that you can better understand how our bodies are designed to live, and how important food, water, fresh air, rest and relaxation, fun and laughter are part of healthy living. This is all given to us by God and contributes to help us maintain a healthy life style.

Recently, I was asked to share my testimony on how I have managed to stay alive and live as healthy as I have since dealing with two (2) bouts of cancer. Cancer for me was a sentence to live and not a sentence to die. Most people from the moment of the diagnoses start dying immediately. This is partly because of all the horror stories they have heard about cancer and the poor survivor rates in our history and because they start trying to eat healthy based on hearsay on not on facts. They pop pills, and take medications prescribed by their doctors who really don't understand the medications themselves, but have been told by the pharmacy industries that this medicine they are selling work for this or that particular ailment.

They forget that the doctors and physicians are practicing medicine. Maybe they are practicing on you. When it comes to cancer or any other disease, doctors depend on the pharmacy industry input to help them solve your problems. This is why many of them will tell you we will try this or that. If this does not work then we will try something else. Sometimes they will give you medications that will soon he recalled shortly after it has been given to you because the side effects are so dangerous.

Remember cancer is a serious, dangerous, and expensive business and being diagnosed with cancer forces us to give our health awareness our undivided attention. In our battle to rid ourselves of this deadly disease, we need to take a closer look at all diseases floating around. It is my personal belief that all sickness and various illnesses are linked. Of course, I am not a doctor I am just stating my opinion based on personal research.

Remember, our immune system is the master brains of our body that controls the well being of our overall health. When this system breaks or becomes unable to perform the duties for which it was created, we are susceptible to all kinds of infectious diseases and any other illnesses that cannot be cured by popping pills, having surgery, or by taking chemotherapy or radiation. To deal effectively with our illness. we must begin with the source of the breakdown that caused us to be sick in the first place.

We seldom question our bodies. we seldom begin by asking our bodies simple questions like, where is this pain coming from? What did I eat that may be causing this discomfort? Why am I so tired? Why can't I sleep at night? Why am I so forgetful? What kind of chest pains are these? What kind of headache is this? Why am I so bloated? Why is my body retaining fluid? Why do my legs and joints hurt? Why am I constipated? Why do I itch? Why am I getting a fever blister? Why is my tongue so white? Why do my eyes look yellow? Why does my stomach feel sick after I eat? Why do I have pains on my side? How did I get kidney stones? The list goes on.........

Not only do we not look at or question our bodies, we seldom examine our spiritual lives. How many times have you wondered or thought about how that penned up anger, malice, bitterness, or jealousies that may have been lurking in our bodies for many years stemming from our past. I want you to wake-up people! And please come with me on a journey that may help you solve some of your health and spiritual problems. And with the help of God, you may be allowed to get back into the swing of life and know that God has it all under control.

Please be reminded that I am not a doctor. Nor am I telling you that you should not see a doctor, but I am telling you this. That it is your responsibility to be mindful of the body that God has given to you to be in charge of You should be an active participant your healing process. So let's get stated.

Start with some active research for yourself. If you don't understand the language or words that your doctor is telling you, look them up. Learn everything there is to know about all the medications you are taking. Stop assuming that your doctor knows and understands the medications they are giving you. They don't, they rely on the drug makers for their knowledge about certain medications. You are responsible to follow-up behind your doctor and read up on all and any medications the doctor has given you. You must know the side effects and learn the risk factors or taking a medication. It may be that the side effects risk is not worth the risk of taking the prescribed medications. Your doctors is not responsible for your lack of knowledge, so keep in mind that this is your body and no one will love, cherish, nourish and care for it the way you will. Someday you will have to answer to God for how you have treated the body he loaned you. So pay attention....!

From The Way It Was To Today

So how can we get back from this place of sickness to living healthy again? I am glad you asked so I can tell you my story. The best way to stay healthy is to never give cancer a chance to start in the first place. Since I am already a cancer patient I had to start at the point of where I was.

Looking back, I can now understand that our bodies were designed by God to heal themselves, therefore one must asks the questions, how did my body get sick in the first place?

Being one of eleven children, visiting the doctor was a very rare occasion and then it was usually for your school shots. My father was not a farmer, but he did raise a garden and we had our own hogs. My mother canned most of the food that daddy had grown in glass jars and at mealtimes we always had a meat and two vegetables.

My grandpa had a big farm plantation where he had many apples, peaches, cherry and plum trees along with various types of vegetables. He had many cattle and horses, pigs and farm animals and he also raised tobacco. My aunt Viola raised cows and supplied our family with lots of homemade butter, milk and buttermilk. Deserts were a luxury and only as a Sunday special. By the way things like cookie, candy and sodas were far and in between. Sweets were not a part of our everyday diet.

When school was out our days were spent doing chores around the house or outside working in the gardens. We would go out to the gardens very early in the morning before the sun got hot. After finishing our chores, we spent the rest of the day playing outside, cleaning the yard, climbing trees, raiding Mr. Sonny's tomatoes garden. Playing cowboys and Indians, building go-carts, exploring the in the woods and damming up the water to make us a swimming pool and going to the brick spring or the hollow spring way out in the woods.

Television was only at night and only after all the dishes were washed, the kitchen cleaned and homework done. When everybody had finished their daily assignments, then we were allowed to watch only one TV show a night before going to bed. At my house the family went to bed at the same time. Meals were fun-times and we always ate together with all eleven children. Our mother and father always ate with us at the table. We were a family around the table and to this day when it is time to eat, the family gathers at the table. Distractions are out, like the TV and Telephone, it was a time of family fellowship.

What a glorious time it was with everybody talking and laughing at something funny that someone had done during the day. Mama disciplined us, but our main discipline came from our daddy. Mama would tell daddy about our bad behavior and he would line-us up and give us a good whooping'. You didn't want to hear mama say, "I'm going to tell your daddy" that was crying time because you knew what was coming next, so the rest of the day, you spent your time trying to be good so mama wouldn't have to tell daddy anything. Sometime it worked and at other times you were in for a good butt whopping.

A funny note. when it was time to disciplined, my brother Douglas whom we called "Buttercup" if he were first in line for a whopping', he would scare the crap out of the rest of us. He was so dramatic with his fake, pretentious and loud crying was so scary, that he made the rest of us standing in line lose heart, because if his was that bad, then you can imagine how bad the rest of ours would be. So the whole line of us little kids was crying madly waiting to get ours. We not only cried for ourselves but we cried for each other we felt sibling pain. Looking back, those whippings were not so bad, it was just how "Buttercup" hollered that made us crazy. After a good whooping, we all slept very well and woke up refreshed the next day. Daddy was never a super big man, but when I was little he looked so big and tall like a giant to me, as I got older I realized that he was small and petite. I sure respected my parents and not just me, all eleven of us did.

We played together, prayed together, had fun together and we loved singing together. We would all get a pot or some kind of pan and beat like drums to make music. Daddy and Mama and the rest of the neighbors would all sit around in their front yards or on their porch and listen to the Pettie Family children while they sang for the entire community. Sometimes, Mr. Jessie, next door, would bring out his guitar and what a time we would have. The whole neighborhood would in their own way get involved.

Being sick back then was a rarity for my family. Doctors were only used in cases where mama's homemade remedies didn't work. The doctor made house calls in our neighborhood and was used in cases like falling out or trees, getting into poison ivy, or some type of unknown fever that required a medical doctor's advice, and of course vaccinations that were required by law.

Daddy and Mama made sure we were healthy by lining us and giving us stuff that would cure anything. Stuff like Cod Liver Oil, Castor Oil, Black Draught and Father John's. Mama made many of her homemade natural rubs and everything else, and anything else that would make us well. My Grandma made a cough syrup with sugar and some kind of liquor. Between my parents and grandparents, we were a pretty healthy bunch. Mama made lye soap which we used for washing clothes, bathing and shampooing our hair. We ate meats like pork, beef, chicken, and fish.

My grandparent from both sides of the family lived to be in their late seventies or early eighties. So what happen that this generation is sicker than ever before? Today we see as much sickness in children as we do in adults. So what is the problem?

When I was a child we always ate a hot breakfast like bacon, eggs, oatmeal, toast, homemade biscuits with jelly or honey, and hot perked coffee and milk. Daddy didn't like us leaving home without having breakfast.

Today's children are fed fast foods for breakfast such as cold cereals, instant oatmeal or grits and pastries. Busy parents on the go may feed their children McDonalds or Burger King, Krystal's, or Chick-Fill-A. This rush causes poor digestion, heart burn and weight gain. Lunches are not much better. Kids eat quickies like pizza, potatoes chips, French fries, cookies, with many carbohydrates and very little fruits and vegetables. Too many children watch TV for hours at a time and very few go outside in the sun to work or play. Dinner is not much different. Fast foods like hamburgers, hotdogs, TV dinners, and Kentucky Fried Chicken make-up many dinner menus. Thus, our families go lacking especially in the area of fellowship and nutrition.

During my childhood parenting was vastly different than today. After learning to read, I remember my father listening to me and correcting me when I made a mistake. Sometimes he would listen to me read "Sally Said" everyday. He was home every night and was the disciplinarian of the family. He always saw to it that we had food, clothing, and shelter. Every pair of shoes I wore he bought for me and the rest of my siblings.

Mama on the other hand was a great nurturer. She gave us lots of love and taught us how to be smart little girls who became smart women. She spent a lot of time teaching the girls while daddy taught the boys hard working skills. Mama was a lover of the Lord. She was also good housekeeper, homemaker, and a good cook. She was fun to be around and beautiful to look at. She prayed a lot for her family and spent much time reading and teaching the bible to her children and the children of the community. She too was a disciplinarian but mostly left the big stuff for daddy.

What made us so healthy then? Why was health not a part of our worries? Why did people live so long and why didn't they get sick? Why did the doctors then make house calls and why were hospitals not such big business, but were really for the sick? I don't remember hearing much about cancer as a child but as I begin to reach adulthood, cancer was on the rise.

Back in the day mothers breast-fed their babies, but now it's old fashion and uncommon, yet breast cancer is on the rise. Why is that? Birth control pills were not heard of in my mother's day, yet today we start girls on birth control medications as young as 10 years old. We place too much of the blame on food and water in regards too many sicknesses, but from where I stand it may be more to it.

So where do we start? Let's look at our DNA system, which I believe is the brain of all cells. How do our bodies get from a health immune system to a weak and sick immune system? I believe that it is from the malnutrition of our bodies. Our bodies were designed to eat. When we eat we feed our cellular system, which sends out healthy cells that works for our bodies. However, when our bodies are malnourished they get sick. Therefore the cells that are designed to keep us healthy start creating havoc.

# PART 4

Being cancer free and staying cancer free requires a lot of prayer, learning and research. Most people think that once they are cancer free, they can go back to what they were doing before. I am here to tell you that taking care of your body is a life-time job. Changing the things that made you sick in the first place is not an easy task. However, it can lead you in a direction that not only can help you, but can help others along the way. God in His wisdom did not put His treasures above the earth. He placed His precious treasures beneath the earth and those who are wise will search for them. This is what it takes with our health; it takes work continual research, and sometimes taking stuff that doesn't taste good and we may we might like. The work is tedious, yet the results can be rewarding by helping to make our journey less painful leading to a road of good health.

Many years ago I use to hear my parents and the older people in the church sing an old hymn call "I wouldn't take anything for my journey now" When I first heard it, it had no meaning to me, just seemed like it was just an old foggy song that they use to sing. But now after surviving cancer for 21 plus years and without taking chemotherapy and still in the land of the living, able to move, breathe and have my being and still alive, I am eternally grateful. I feel like a sister in our church who always says, "I am blessed beyond telling." God is so good, great, and awesome and more than any words can describe.

While taking this journey you got to remain prayerful asking God to guide you every step of the way. While He is leading you He will be to you like the clouds that lead the children of Israel through the wilderness. He made you, and He knows you better than any person on the earth. He knows about every cell in your body and how each are designed to work. He knows when a foreign substance is in your body and how to attack that which does not belong.

Before asking God to heal you, make sure you are prepared spiritually to come into His presence. No one can whose heart is not right So examine yourself and see if there are things that may keep God from your healing you, such things as anger malice, bitterness, jealously, lying, and wickedness. God is Holy and must be approached with holiness and a pure heart.

Keep in mind it is not always God's will to heal us here on earth. Sometimes we are chosen to suffer, yet we still can trust Him in our pain and suffering. Just keep in mind that no one will die before their appointed time. We are all appointed a death date and the best way to be ready when that day come is to have a personal relationship with the Lord Jesus Christ. You can do that by trusting Him right now as your personal Savior.

After trusting Him as your personal Savior, begin worshiping and serving Him. Learn more about Him and praise Him for the things He has already done for you. For instance, it is a blessing to know that you have cancer, because now you can do something about it. He could have kept you in the dark and allowed you to be blind about it until it was too late. Instead of complaining start, giving Him praise for knowing what going on inside of you. Now you can do something about it. Therefore, no matter what is going on in your life learn to give Him Praise. God inhabits the praises of His people.

Now that you have gotten that settle, you can now start treating your problem. First, look at all the scriptures that pertain to healing. Note that some healing comes by the Will of God. If the Lord wills that you be healed, you will be healed no matter what. Make sure you are asking for His will to be done in your life. Demanding God to heal you is not the answer. He is not a toy that you can use. Sometimes he says yes. Sometimes He say wait, and at other time it is no. No matter what His will for you is, be patient and let Him do what He has planned for you. He knows the plans He has for you. He knows your todays and tomorrows. So let the God have his way in your current condition. It is important that you remain humble depending solely upon Him! Be open to what He is showing you and follow His lead.

# On the Road to Recovery

*Healing yourself with natural herbs*

Taking charge of your health is the first step in getting healthy.

Getting sick was not in our plans. Sometimes we wonder just how we got there. We know that we are feeling sick, and sometimes that the feeling of tiredness and the aches and pains are just a normal part of growing old. Many of us never ask the important question of "where is this pain coming from and why am I feeling so tired"? We assume that we may have a yeast infection or that rapid weight lost, extreme thirst and frequent urinations are just a part of life. By paying attention to our bodies, we may find that we can live a quality life of that is pleasing and meaningful. Natural herbs can provide great assistant in getting healthy. However, before you start taking natural herbs, make sure you check with your health care provider. Also make sure that you research each herb before you take it, some herbs clash with others. it is my desire that this study will be helpful to you in your quest in becoming healthy. May what you learn will be shared with someone else who is going through some of the same health issues. We are now ready to begin our quest to help ourselves in becoming healthy.

## The Best Herbs to use for Diabetes:

If you are a diabetic and are having problems controlling your blood sugar, it is time to get your blood sugar under control. You can do this learning the type of herbs that will aid you in giving your body the assistance it needs. Diabetes is a very serious and dangerous problem that can affect all of your major organs. It can lead to amputations, have a negative effect on the liver, lungs and heart and other vital organs. If you are Type II diabetic you can get better control of it with certain herbs. Below are lists of herbs that may help you manage and even prevent diabetes. When you are grocery shopping, you may want to start including and introducing these herbs in your healing regiment of healing. If you use insulin you may want to concur with your physician before putting these herbs into your body.

# Teas

Bitter <u>Melon</u> Tea (Note: stay within dosage suggested if not it may cause abdominal pains and diarrhea).

Burdock Tea (has many healing agents including healing cancer).

<u>Carob</u> Tea (drinking Carob Tea after a meal can help slow the release of sugar in the blood stream and help ward off craving for sugar and desserts)

Cinnamon & Hone Tea

Green Black and White Tea

Gymnema Leaf Tea

Hyssop Tea

Tropical Morning Garb Tea

## For Sweeteners:

Stevia (reduces the intake of Sugar)

Stevia Leaf Sweetener

## Tonic:

Spicy and Sassy Blood Tonic

For Swelling:

Bromelain Capsules

Butcher Broom

Blueberry Leaves (aids in capillary integrity, free radicals damage, and it improves the vascular system

## Yellow Dock

Fenugreek Seed Capsules (contains anti-diabetic properties)

Fresh Garlic Cloves (lowers blood glucose levels)

Onions (prevents insulin's destruction)

Turmeric (helps with Inflammation and many other ailments)

Ginkgo Biloba (helps with diabetic neuropathy leg and nerve pains)

Cinnamon (triples insulin's sufficiency, helps in weight control and lessens the risk of heart disease)

Barberry (a liver tonic) Bilberry (helps with cataracts and retinopathy)

Sage (drinking sage on an empty stomach reduces blood sugar)

Natural Herbs

And God said, "See, I have given you every herb that yields seed which is on the face of all the earth, and every tree whose fruit yields seed; to you it shall be for food. Also to every beast of the earth, to every bird of the air arid to everything that creeps on the earth, in which there is life, I have given every green herb for food and is was so. Then God saw everything that He had made and indeed it was very good. So evening and morning were the sixth day." Genesis 1:29-31

Many people may be asking the question why write about herbs? My answer is simple. In 1995 I was diagnosed with Uterine Cancer and five years later was diagnosed with Lung Cancer. I was divested because I was given less than 5 years to live. I needed answers and needed them fast. My doctor immediately recommended an Oncologist to be in charge of my case. He insisted that the only cure for me was through radiation and chemotherapy. I felt confused, frighten and uncomfortable with what he told me. He didn't offer me much hope. So I did what I knew best, I cried out to the Lord.

Moreover, at the time of my diagnoses I was a student at Crossroads Institute of Biblical Studies. I had been studying the Word of God for many years but I never thought that cancer would be my test. I had a potential death sentence hanging over me...

---


At Crossroads, I had taken a class in theology that studied the decrees of God. One of the decrees that stood out in my mind was "it is rendered certain, that in eternity pass, (before the foundations of the world) that what God decreed for me would come pass in time." So whatever God planned for me before I came into this world was going to happen to me and there was nothing I could do to stop it! My current situation took me by surprise but it did not take God by surprise.

At the church where I attend my pastor and husband had just finished teaching on the book of Job. In that book I learned that before Satan could touch Job he had to first go to God and get permission. So I took that literally. I believed God and started seeking answers in His Word. God gave me some powerful Help through His Word as it became more real and personal to me.

Satan attacks Job's character. "Now there was a day where the sons of God came to present themselves before the Lord, and Satan also come among them. And the Lord said to Satan, from where do you come"? So Satan answered the Lord and said "from going to and fro on the earth and walking back and forth on it." Then the Lord said to Satan "have you considered my servant Job, that there is none like him on the earth, a blameless and upright man. One who fears God and shuns evil"?

I realized that it was God who pointed Job out to Satan. And it was God who said to Satan that he could afflict Job, but with limits! Satan had to go to God and get permission to touch me. It was a real eye-opener, for it made me wants to dig deeper and know more!! I also learned that God is not the author of confusion or disorder in 1 Corinthians 14:33 it says "For God is not the author of confusion"; this hit me like a ton of bricks, because I felt confused about taking chemotherapy confused me...

What confused me was how something that potentially poisons my system was supposed to heal me. I didn't understand how chemotherapy could kill the good cells as well as the bad cells and at the same time cause me to get well. I couldn't understand how a medicine that was used for taking down my immunize system would also rebuild it. It didn't make a lot of since to me. So I chose to trust God.

If God made every cell in my body, certainly he knows how to heal me if that is His will.

I would like to introduce you to some of the herbs I used to start my journey of getting healthy.

These formulas helped me here is a brief description of how they work. It is also helpful to keep an accurate record of how they are helping you. It is important to understand how to take herbal remedies safely.

**Here are a few suggestions and safety tips that may be helpful as you begin your adventure in natural remedies.**

1. Know and understand the plants that you are taking. Especially look at the benefits and the side effects.

2. Make sure you understand your diagnosis. Find out whether the herbs that you have chosen will work for the type of sickness or disease you may have.

3. Don't just take herbs because your friends or relatives told you about it.

4. Research each herb.

5. Study the history of a particular herb and learn whether it can cause other problems like heart disease, diabetes, cancer or other major illness.

6. Know when to avoid a particular herb and how long you can take it.

7. Learn the side effects whether they cause:

   a. Blurred Visions

   b. Diarrhea

   c. Increased Salvation

   d. Irregular heartbeat

   e. Nausea

   f. Numberless and tingling of the arms and legs

   g. Numbness around the mouth

   h. Slow heartbeat

   i. Throat Closure

   j. Vomiting

   k. Weakness

8. How much is a dose.

9. Learn how that herb interacts with another herb or drugs you are taking.

10. Study the reason why people are using this herb and see whether it is a benefit.

    a. Fever

    b. Headache

c. High blood pressure

d. Inflammation

e. Severe stabbings pains

11. Make sure you know that death can occur by your own abuse of herbs.

**The collection of herbs that I will be listing is the ones, which I have personally studied and used. Let's begin...**

## Aloe Vera

*The Aloe Vera Plant has a history of over 5000 years*

The Aloe Vera plant is a part of the Lily family which is in the same family of onions and garlic. It can be used both internal and external. The Aloe Vera Leaf is filled with a clear gel-like substance that contains at least 99% of water. There are approximately 200 active components in this plant which includes vitamins, mineral amino acids, enzymes, polysaccharide and fatty acids.

The vitamins and minerals in Aloe Vera includes vitamins, A,C, E, folic acid, choline, B1, B2, B3 (niacin) and B6 It also contains B12, calcium, magnesium, chromium, selenium sodium, iron, potassium, copper and manganese.

## Vitamin A:

*Important for Eyesight:*

Vitamin A is good for the skin, hair and mucous membranes, which helps to keep them in good condition. It also strengthens the immune system, develops bone, teeth, epithelial cell situated on the inside and outside of the body cavities such as the nose, mouth, throat, lungs, stomach intestines, and urinary tract. It has powerful antioxidants.

You can get vitamin A from foods such as oranges; add yellow vegetables, fruits (e.g., nectarines, cantaloupe, and carrots), spinach, broccoli, butter, eggs, milk, fish oil, liver, beef, pork, chicken, turkey and lamb.

## Vitamin B:

Consist of several vitamins B1, B2, B6, and B12, biotin, folic acid, niacin and pantothenic acid. The reason you need Vitamin B is helps the metabolism B Vitamins moves red blood through the body which contains oxygen. The importance of this process is the protein synthesis and the creation of energy. You get your B vitamins from whole grains (e.g. oats and wheat) peas, beans, leafy green vegetables, citrus fruits, seafood, eggs and dairy products such as milk, yogurt and meat.

## Vitamin C, call ascorbic acid:

*It is water soluble with antioxidant properties*

The reason you need it is because it is a part of the collagen production and gives strength to bone cartilage, ligaments, tendon, muscles, teeth and blood vessels.

It also protects gums and muscle. It helps to speed up the healing of wounds. It also prevents soluble vitamins life like A, E, and other fatty acids from oxidizing which keep the skin healthy. It also reduces damage to the body from toxic substances and chemicals. Speeds up, wound healing. Prevents soluble vitamins life like A and E and other fatty acids from oxidizing which keeps the skin healthy. It also reduces damage to body from toxic substances and chemicals.

You get some of your vitamin citrus fruits (e.g. oranges, lemons) and in other fruits (e.g. cantaloupe, strawberries and vegetables (e.g. broccoli, tomatoes and cabbage).

## Vitamin D: A fat soluble vitamin

The reason you need it is because part of calcium aids in phosphorus absorption from the intestine and in bone formation. Vitamin D also regulates calcium movement from bone to blood and vice versa. It also helps in preventing osteoporosis.

Eggs yolks, milk and fish oil, and cod liver oil provides a good dose of this vitamin. Sunlight and ultraviolet fight can help the body synthesis vitamin D.

Aloe Vera is rich in amino acids and fatty acid the building block of protein.

Amino acids are the building blocks of protein

Aloe, contains three plant sterols, which are important fatty acids.

These include HCL cholesteric which lowers fats in the blood

Campestral and-sitosterol is helpful in reducing symptoms of allergies and acid indigestion.

## Aloe Vera is an Adaptogen:

It helps with digestion and aid in detoxification, alkalizes the body, aids in cardiovascular health, helps boost the immune system, and it is good for the skin.

Aloe Vera is a disinfectant, anti-biotic, anti-microbial, germicidal, anti-bacteria; anti-septic, anti-fungal and anti-viral herb, that helps to treat fungal and viral infections. It also helps reduce inflammation, weight loss-a secondary effect.

The reason the people use this herb is because it helps with acne, arthritis's asthma, bleeding, blindness, bursitis, cancer common cold, colitis, inflammation or the large intestine constipation, depression, diabetics, glaucoma, hemorrhoids, lack of menstruation, secure, skin conditions abrasions, cuts infection and much more.

## Asparagus: Loaded with five powerful benefits

1. It is loaded with nutrients: A good source of fiber, folate, and vitamins A.C.E. and K. It is also has chromium and trace minerals that enhances the ability of insulin to transport glucose for the bloodstream into the cells.

2. This herbaceous plant—along with avocado, kale and Brussel sprouts—is particularly rich source of glutathione a detoxifying compound that helps break down carcinogens and other harmful agents as like free radicals. This is why eating asparagus may help protect against and fight certain forms of cancer such as bone, breast, colon, larynx and lung cancers.

3. Asparagus is packed with antioxidants, ranking among the top fruits and vegetables for its ability to neutralize cell-damage free radicals. This according to preliminary research may help slow the aging process.

4. Another anti-aging property is it may help our brains fight cognitive decline. Leafy greens, asparagus deliver folate, which works with vitamin B12 which is found in fish, poultry, meat and dairy to help repairs cognitive skills. If you are 50 plus, be sure you are getting enough B12; your ability to absorb it decreases with age.

5. Asparagus contains high levels of amino acid asparagine, which serve as a natural diuretic. It increases urination which helps rid the body of excess salts. This is especially beneficial for people who suffer from edema accumulations and high

blood pressure. Asparagus is loaded with vitamins minerals. It is also a diuretic and an excellent source of vitamin B6.

Asparagus contains high level of beta-carotene, vitamin c, vitamin E, vitamin K, thiamin, riboflavin, rutin, niacin, folic acid, iron phosphorus, copper potassium, selenium and manganese. It is rich in dietary fiber. It helps control diabetes, acts as a diuretic, prevents kidney stone and reduces the rich or neural tube defects in babies. You can even make an asparagus, Spanish & fruit smoothie take;

1 cup of fresh baby Spanish

4 asparagus spears trimmed

1 cup of cantaloupe cut-up

I Grannie Smith Apple with skin, cored and cut up

34 cup of almond unsweetened milk

1 tablespoon of organic honey

1 cup of Ice cubes

Blend ingredients until smooth, poor into a glass and enjoy

The Benefits of Castor Oil

## What is Castor Oil?

Castor Oil is a very pale liquid that is extracted for the castor seed. It is anti-inflammatory and anti-oxidant oil which has been use for centuries for medicinal and therapeutic benefits. It also has been used in cosmetic, soaps, textiles, medicines, massage oil and many other everyday products. It has been it has been used both internally and externally for many years can strengthen the immune system. Here are some of the benefits of this great oil.

## It can be used for:

Pain from Arthritis and Rheumatism

Hair Loss

Constipation

Gastrointestinal Problems

Migraines

Yeast Infections

Multiple Sclerosis

Cerebral Palsy

Menstrual disorders

Acne

Alleviate Colic in Babies

Hemorrhoid treatment

Beautiful Nails (hands and feet)

Message Oil

Insomnia treatment

Starches

Relieves sore muscles

Split Ends

Healthy Lips

Alethea's Foot

Sunburn

Removes warts and skin tags

Age spots

Improves the Immune system

Helps with mild surface tumors

Helps with the Lymphatic System and Liver

Joint Pains

Thickens Eyebrows and Lashes

Scalp Infections

Hair Darkening

Promotes Hair Growth

Skin Pigmentation

Castor Oil can even be used as a disinfectant. It helps with for ringworms, fungal skin infections, minor cuts and scrapes. It has anti-itch and pain relieving proper-ties, and can be used topically. Castor oil fades scars and stretch marks. It acts as a moisturizer that helps with wrinkles and fine line and all sorts or skin problems can be helped with this product.

## Castor oil can aid in arthritis and Joint Pain:

Castor oil is great remedy for treating arthritis. Its anti-inflammatory properties make it ideal massage for relieving joint pain, nerve inflammation and sore muscle: Here is a step by step guide for using it for joint pain.

## For Joint Pains:

Take a piece of flannelette or a soft cotton fabric and fold it into squares. Soak it in castor oil, press out excess oil and place it on the affected joint and cover with a plastic wrap. Place a hot water bottle or heating pad on this—the plastic will save the bottle from getting oily. Leave it on for an hour. Keep the oil pad in a zip lock bag and store in the fridge—can be used again. This process should be repeated twice a week for positive results. Also, drink two spoonful of castor oil mixed with water to ease relentless rheumatoid arthritis. Castor oil packs usually provide relief from joint and tissue pains.

## The-Benefits of Olive Oil:

## What is Olive Oil?

Olive Oil is a fat obtains for the fruit of the Olea-European (olive tree). It is a traditional crop of the Mediterranean Region where whole olives are pressed to produce olive oil. It is rich in menstruated fatty acids which are major component of the Mediterranean diet. People in that area have a longer life expectancy and low risk of heart disease, high blood pressure and stroke. This oil is also used in cosmetics, medicine, cooking and soaps.

## What are the health benefits of olive oil?

Olive Oil Protects against breast cancer, may

reduce breast cancer risks

Reduce the risk of Alzheimer's disease

Helps to prevent skin cancer

Helps to prevents cardiovascular disease

Helps lower hypertensions (high blood pressure), stroke, and high blood  cholesterol and triglyceride levels.

Helps reduce inflammation

Aids in the digestive health benefits

Support bone health

Cognitive benefits (especially among older adults)

Aids in anti-cancer benefits

Helps prevent strokes

Helps maintain healthy cholesterol level

Helps prevent acute pancreatic

Protects the-liver

Protects ulcerative colitis

Helps with high blood pressure

Helps with diabetes

Helps with Obesity

Helps with Rheuetorid Arthritist

Helps with Osteoporosis

Olive Oil tries to reduce the risk of Type 2 Diabetes

## Extra Virgin Olive Oil Dip:

1/2 teaspoon Oregano

1 teaspoon of basil

1 teaspoon of Rosemary

1 teaspoon of Kosher Salt (according to your taste)

Freshly ground black pepper

I pinch of Red Pepper Flakes

2 cloves of fresh garlic minced

1 cup of extra virgin olive oil

Mix all the dry spices and the crushed garlic stir to combine and moisten the herbs. Pour Olive Oil over herbs and serve with fresh bread.

## Olive Oil Dip for Italian Bread:

1/4 cup of Olive Oil

5 Cloves of fresh garlic

2 tablespoons balsamic vinegar

2 tablespoons parmesan cheese

1 tablespoon of oregano

Black pepper to taste

Serve with French bread. It also makes a good salad dressing.

Getting healthy and staying healthy is not only a learning experience, but it is a life time of research, trial and error. It is my desire that all who read this edition will continue to get healthy and stay healthy. It is also important to that as you learn new information, you will be willing to share with others what you have learned.

Thank you for trusting me with my research and may God richly bless you with a long healthy life.

# PART 5

# APPENDIX

## The Faithfulness of the Lord

Oh Lord, you are still faithful, loving and kind. I am so thankful that you are mindful of me a sinner and a wretch undone, one filled with my own little world of wants.

Help me Lord to take my eyes off myself and to put them on you. Looking back, maybe that's why you allowed me to get cancer. It could be that I need this time to get to know you better. It has shown me that I needed to pay more attention to my vessel; this body, this temple that you have loaned me to dwell in during my stay upon this earth. Life is precious, very short, and is to be used for your glory.

Cancer and all of its woes can really let you know how precious every moment of life that God has given you. If God has blessed you to be a cancer survivor you are probably a person who also sees life a lot differently.

Before my cancer and before my body started giving me the warning signs, I never had time to live. I only existed. I was too busy to stop and smell the roses. Now that I have cancer, my life has changed and now I find the time to enjoy the many precious moments I have received from you. I enjoy quite moment and the precious time you have given me to enjoy, see, feel and times and the wonderful and beautiful elements of the world around me. I have more meaningful and precious moments to communicate, love and be loved by my family my husband Donald and my daughter Leni. It's like God has given me a new lease on life and allowed me to put the priorities of my life in its proper perspective. And live today for tomorrow is not promised. I can now more enthusiastically enjoy the small things such as the children of the church and to pray with my thoughts about them during the day.

Life is a blessing and one of my greatest blessings was cancer, because it taught me to get my life in order. It helped me to rid myself of some of the rocks such as anger, malice, bitterness, jealously and anything else

I was carrying. You see, I believe that cancer is not a death sentence, it is a sentence to live. Cancer has caused me to appreciate every small detail of life and not to be over-burden with the cares of this world. It helped me to look-up and put my faith and priorities on God.

As cancer survivors, we can acquire contentment with life that we have never had before. Without all the distractions, our praise and worship can be more genuine. Our family time is valued, our views of the world changes, because now, we can find good and shun some of the evil that so easily besets us. Our time is more valuable and we realized that we must be doing what God wants us to do. We are no longer consumed by the petty things. Our lives are no longer tied to our televisions sets and bogged down with the cares of this world. We have some living to do.

Could it be that we have gotten a taste of heaven right here on earth? The truth about cancer is that it really does change how you view life. Our thoughts are hopefully now more heavenward. We know that we are preparing for a journey that only God can give us the help we need for us to survive. God can give us a peace in a difficult situation that only He can give. He leads us to truths that can transform our lives in a way that will help us live through this amazing life experience. Only God knows the plans He has for me. The end results of all our lives are in His hands. The only thing we can do is to trust and go along for the ride in hopes that all will be well with us because of our faith in His son.

So let us strive to have peace, contentment, and enjoy the rest of our days loving and staying in harmony with God. King Solomon wrote in the book of Ecclesiastes that we should "eat, drink, and be merry." Maybe cancer was what God wanted to use let me know that I've only begun to know the real reason why I was born in the first place.

### My Quest for Healing:

My quest for healing has led me in many directions searching for truth to make me well again. I have read various books, healing magazines, thousands of articles about cancer, I have searched the World Wide Web, listen and interview hundreds of cancer patient, found out their likes and dislikes, and asked many questions of my doctors and alternative medicine people.

I have suffered much pain and I have learned how to make my own pain relief. I call it ER Pain Relief. I came about because of my broken ribs after lung cancer surgery. I was in so much pain one day until I asked to Lord to show me how to get rid of this pain and he gave me this formula. It really helped me. Also, being on so much medication I also lost my hair so I asked God to teach me how to re-grow my hair and he gave me the know how to develop a product I call ER Healthy Hair. My hair is now below my shoulders. It was once very brittle, wiry, breaking, and hard. It came out and left me looking like a plucked chicken. It is now healthy and silky. Every time I comb or brush my hair I thank God for hair.

I have inquired of physicians, and talked with many people who have suffered with cancer. I have gone to a naturopath and have enrolled in a college that teaches natural medicine. It is my prayer that all who reads this book will be helped. I pray that in your reading you will get a new outlook on a new life. I hope the context of this book will bring you hope, healing, happiness and peace. I pray that as you start your journey to healing that God will grant you healing and that he will also lead you to a personal relationship with His Son, Jesus Christ. Without Jesus I could not have survived this ordeal.

It is also my prayer that as you read and glance through these pages you will find a few helpful hints that will lead you in a better understand of your situation. It is also my desire that as you read and increase your knowledge, you too will write down your own experiences and helps that will allow others to share in your health secrets. No one has all the answers, but who knows, one lay person might just be the one who finds a cure for cancer after all. Who knows how God will use us to help people.

If you would like to reach me, or if I can help in any way please feel free to contact me. My address is *5158* Sand Hill Circle, N. Lizella, GA 31052 or you may reach me at (478) 935-2948.

Thank you so much for investing in my book.

*Evelyn Reid*

### *Attitudes To Avoid And To Embrace:*

After learning of sickness in my body, I found I had a lot of pent up anger and bitterness which may have been a contributing factor in causing a lot of my sickness. I also discovered by reading a book by Rev. Rick Warren, *How to Study the Bible,* that I had been harboring things that the bible tells us not to. Maybe these hints will help you release some of your frustration so you too can get healed. I believe in getting rid of some of my hidden rocks (such as anger, malice, bitterness, and etc.) that I had been caring. It made a big difference in my body that was the beginning of my healing process. I hope it will help you too.

Instead of anger try love.

Instead of violence try compassion.

Instead of harsh or harmful speech try speech that uplifts people.

Instead of conceit try cleanliness.

Instead of speaking ill of others try charity and giving.

Instead of egotism try being humble before the Lord God.

Instead of dishonesty try honesty.

Instead of coveting another's wealthy try praising the progress of others.

Instead of being disrespectable try showing respect.

Instead of being negative, try being positive.

Try showing self-control and moderation in all areas of your life.

Make your life simple. Have some fun. Laugh and enjoy the small stuff.

Meditate on God's word; it will help you figure out how to live.

## *Positive Qualities:*

It is really necessary to get your attitude right when you are asking God to heal you. Being angry with God and staying mad by having temper tantrums and fits will not aid you in your healing process. When you understand these qualities, it may be the beginning of your healing process just as it was for me. I found them to give me a humbleness that I needed for God to heal and use me.

I am to be a servant; I must serve others just as Jesus Christ came to serve me.

I must be honest and must confess anything that will hinder me from being healed.

I must have humility. I must be humble enough that God can use me and not be selfish in sharing what He has done for me.

I must have determination. I must have a will to live and not give up just because I am having a bad day or got some more bad news.

I must be diligence to seek every opportunity to learn all that I can to help myself.

I must have faithfulness, to hold on to my faith no matter what is happening knowing that in the end God will do right by me.

I must have availability, to avail myself to knowledge and keep my immune system healthy by being available to learn all I can about myself, and to be willing to seek out much council and many opinions.

I must be teachable and not be a know it all. It is very unattractive because there is always somebody out there that is smarter in this area than me.

I must be forgiving and be willing to forgive past hurts. This forgiveness must be genuine. The bible says forgive that your heavenly father will forgive you. Don't hold anything in your heart that will hinder you from being heal. Search yourself.

I must be generous and not withhold any information that will help someone else with the same problems I am presently experiencing.

You must have loyalty. Be loyal to what you know and don't change with every wind that blows your way. If something works keep using it. It may be the key that will save your life.

You must be fair. Be fair with yourself and others and it will pay off in the long run.

You must have a spirit of cooperativeness. Don't try to walk this path alone. Cooperate with those who are trying to help you especially your doctors, family, and friends. Don't be defiant.

You must be sincere. Be sincere about what's going on with you and asks for help when needed.

You must have contentment. Be content with yourself and don't allow restlessness to creep up in your spirit. You just didn't get sick in one day. Sickness was lurking around in your body for a long time before it reared its ugly head. In your watch, remain patient because God maybe healing you one day at a time. In the mean time, lay down in green pastures, for God knows that you need this time to rest.

## Negative Qualities

By understanding these negative qualities and getting rid of them may be your key to getting better. See if you have any and start working on them right away. Remember you want to get well.

Laziness will keep you in bed and waiting for other to serve you. Get up and get moving it will help you regain your strength.

A critical spirit will cause others who may serve you stay away from you because in your eyes, they can't do anything right.

Pride is usually the last to go, it can kill you, and can cause you to isolate yourself from others and not to seek help when you need it. It can bring you to your knees if you don't get in check. Be careful and don't let your pride overtake you.

Selfishness can be when you are only thinking about yourself and forgetting about others who may care for you.

Unfaithfulness can cause you to cheat and bring damage to yourself and others. Cheating does not necessary mean cheating on a love one but being unfaithful to God as well.

Disrespectfulness can be hurtful especially to those who have your best interest at heart. Be careful that you don't disrespect the hands that may have to feed you and give you a bath during you illness.

Rebelliousness can be hateful and very unbecoming especially when it is done in a verbal, nasty and public way.

Gossip can be like a tongue on fire spurting out all kinds of evil to someone who may be doing you some good.

Being unloving can cause people stay away from you.

Dishonesty is like stealing, telling lies, and using people for your own gain. Be careful and aware of the type of behavior you are displaying.

Impatience can lead to much disappointment. Be willing to wait on the Lord for he knows when you have had enough. He will raise you up at the proper time. So be patience.

Worry can turn your hairs gray and change nothing about your situation.

Fearfulness can overtake you and cause you not to be much good to yourself or others. God has not given you the spirit of fear, but the spirit of power, love and a sound mind.

Lustfulness can cause you to stumble.

Bitterness can be deeply rooted and come up with a vengeance.

There are many other character qualities found in the scripture, but these should get you started on your way to healing. Take a good look at your attitude. It may be a key in your healing process.

### Pay Attention to Your Body:

Your body has a built in warning system that will let you know when something is wrong. So pay attention, it may save your life.

Listen, your body may be speaking:

- Don't just take a pill to cover up pain, asks questions?

- Where is this pain coming from?

- What is causing it?

- Am I under stress?

- Why isn't over the counter medicine working?

Be aware of your own body, in other words know your body:

- Make sure you are having proper bowel eliminations.

- Check your body for lumps, knots or moles.

- Don't just assume anything.

- See a doctor.

- Don't diagnose your own case.

- Know your medications and the side effects.

- Know what medicines cannot be taken with over the counter medications.

- Take your medications dilligently

- Read the labels; don't just take it because your doctor gave it to you. Know what kinds of reactions you are having and know when and how to get help if necessary.

- Get second and third opinions.

- Talk to others who have gone through similar experiences (especially those with positive attitudes and survival techniques).

- Listen to your body.

- Get you proper rest.

- Take your medications with water to prevent allergic reactions.

- If you get a rash or start to swell get help immediately. If you have shortness of breath or temporary blindness, seek professional help immediately.

- Take proper dose amounts of medications, (don't over medicate).

- Have emergency numbers available.

- Wear identifications bracelets so that your problem can be resolved easily.

- Know your blood type (it can save your life).

- To prevent AIDS or some other illness, store up your own blood in case of emergency before having surgery.

- Follow your doctors especially if you trust them.

- Keep a diary of the foods you eat, and know the foods that may cause a reaction in your body which make you sick. Be able to explain if necessary what happens when you eat this kind of food?

- Never take a prescription that has another person's name on it.

- Get a pill box to help you remember your medications and the hours to take the recommended dose.

- Educate yourself on your condition and be ready to explain what you know to your doctor.

- Don't assume your doctors know everything. Do some investigating on your own then you can help your doctor better assess your condition.

- Watch out for rashes or patches on the skin. Your body may be giving you a sign or warning of some kind that an infection maybe lurking around in your body.

- Make sure that the foods you are eating are not clashing with your medication which may cause an allergic reaction in some way.

- Boils are a sign of some kind of infection in your body,

- Don't wear clothing that is uncomfortable or too tight, it can cause problems for the skin and yeast infections.

- Pay attention to your feet and check them often for sores or infections.

- Don't assume that all stomach or chest pains is gas. Don't blame all of your symptoms on gas.

- Pay attention to any changes in your body and if there is blood in the urine or stool, seek professional help immediately.

- The more you pay attention to your body and know it well the better your chances of survival.

### *A Few More Do's and Don'ts:*

1. Do let a cancer person talk about dying if they want to or feel need to do so. Dying can be a positive experience when the families are on one accord and especially if that person is saved.

2. Death and dying of a cancer patient should not be hidden from children because it is a fact in life. They need to settle in their minds that a parent, grandparent, sister or brother is going home to be with the Lord (assuming that person is saved). Don't be afraid to asked a dying person if they are saved. It may feel uncomfortable but you will be offering that person eternal life.

3. Don't pretend that death is not real. It can leave an empty void in the lives of those living if it is not handled properly.

4. Don't plan for a sad obituary. Let it tell the good, positive, and wonderful things about that person that can be remembered. It's not just their education and employment it is much than

that that needs to be represented. For example, "he/she thought they were the greatest singer on the planet, yet he/she couldn't hold a tune."

5.  Don't put all of your insurance money into a funeral to impress others. Keep those finances for yourself or family members who may need it later.

6.  If you are the spouse of a dying person, don't get involved with another person before the death of your loved one. It can be devastating to that person.

7.  Do have compassion for the grieving family.

*Preventive Methods That May Save Your Life:*

Preventive method of foods that have disease prevention properties:

**Inflammation:**

Juice up your joints with Turmeric!

-   Turmeric cuts down on inflammation and reduces your sugar intake. Be sure to exercise because it keeps your joints working. Green leafy vegetables fight free radicals. Free radicals in the body can cause havoc on your joints. Don't wait! Here is you chance to begin these preventive methods now.

-   Turmeric also helps with annoying infections in your nose, throat, and lungs.

-   Turmeric disposes of bad digestion and aids in the digestive process. It also fights harmful bacteria which can wreck havoc in your mouth, stomach, and other parts of the digestion track.

- Turmeric: will help dissolved undesirable fats in your body instead of allowing them to accumulate. This antioxidant is supreme for it gobbles up free radicals and promotes your blood vessels. It is antibacterial and is always good for the heart to cut down on infectious causing bacteria in the system. It is good for your heart and if you eat turmeric regularly it may be preventive in eliminating cancer.

Turmeric protects your DNA. It stimulates the enzymes that gets rid of toxins and protects healthy cells against cancer. It can help keep down inflammation and helps to make nutrients better at fighting cancer as they are naturally fighting bacteria. It is a good way to look at and address all kinds of side effects of Chemotherapy.

*Energy Booster and Stress Reducers Mints:*

Energy boasting supplements aid in the creation of a steady, stable velocity that you can depend on throughout the day.

You do not want energy extremes like caffeine that gives you highs and lows. Energy extremes take a toll on our well being. An example would he our blood sugar balance which could have a roller coaster effect of our hyperglycemic and hypoglycemic. This roller coaster effect can lead us to being unstable, uneducated, and unequipped to get a handle on your day. This can lead to various chronic health problems.

Here is a list of supplements that may help you build your energy life.

Vitamins B12

Flax Seed Oil

Vitamins E

Grapes Seed Oil

Bar leans Greens

Graviola

Vitamins B6

*Why Enzymes Need To Be Part Of Your Daily Diet:*

In my research, I found that enzyme deficiencies are the main cause for a long list of illnesses that occur in our society. It has caused a lot of health issues that can lead to death if not taken care of as soon as possible. Enzyme deficiencies are found in many of the following illness: cancer, heart disease, arthritis, chronic fatigue, various pains, allergies, migraines, multiple sclerosis and many other conditions.

Enzymes can clear up many digestive problems like irritable bowel syndrome, excessive gas, bloating, diarrhea, constipation, leaky gut syndrome, and yeast infections. Enzymes are in my personal regiment and I also recommended that my family members also use them. By my personal experience, I can say for sure they work.

What enzymes are and how they work:

An Enzyme is a catalyst-a chemical that causes a reaction to happen or to happen faster. Enzymes are a type of protein. Enzymes and proteins are made up of amino acids. More than 3,000 enzymes have been identified in the body. Digestive enzymes play an important role in the way our body functions. These enzymes allow the food that you eat to be use to build your own bone and tissue or to burn for energy.

As the body grows older it loses a lot, and one of the things it loses is its ability to make enzymes, which puts us at risk to have majors illness and/or other medical problems which seems to come with age. So, if you want to speed up your aging process don't take enzymes which are a vital nutrient that will help us stay young, healthy and feeling better.

Some of the leading enzyme researchers say cancer and circulation diseases are profoundly related. They note that cancer patients suffer blood clots (thromboses) and patients with blood clots tend to have cancer. For more information on this subject you may want to refer to a book by Dr. Cichoke called Enzyme & Enzyme Therapy.

Lactose Intolerance is when the body doesn't make lactase, the enzyme you need to digest lactose, a sugar found in milk. The symptoms of milk intolerance are abdominal pains cramps, bloating, diarrhea, and gas, pimples and skin rashes.

Enzymes Answer to Heart and Circulation: Suggest that enzymes are one way to possibly to treat pain and inflammation in the body which also reduces cholesterol, break up blood clots that may cause heart attacks and strokes, and thins the blood. They may work as well as or better than some prescription blood thinners:

Try enzymes for three (3) months (take before or after eating) it may solve many of your digestive problems and save you many trips to the doctor. I did.

*Helpful Hints to Help You:*

- Rebuild Your Immune System
- Know What Your Problems Are
- And Equip You To Talk To Your Doctor

**Abdominal Pain & Constipation:**

Can be nagging and upsetting especially when you don't know where it is coming from or the reason it is happening. This was one of my first warning signs that I didn't pay any attention to. Theses pains can be from mild to severe, dull or sharp, acute to chronic. Acute pain is sudden pain, while chronic pain can be constant or pain that recurs over time.

Abdominal pain may be related to one of the following symptoms, which can cause the stomach much discomfort and pain like constipation, gastroenteritis, lactose intolerance, menstrual cramps and peptic ulcers. Too bad that I had to spend a fortune before I found out this knowledge. I was going from one specialist to another spending money I didn't have.

Before starting any treatment or herbal use that anyone recommends you should know what kind of abdominal pain you are dealing with. For instance constipation may result from not drinking enough fluids, or eating dietary fiber, or being active or by misusing laxatives.

Some of the signs of constipation are: hard stools (not being able to pass stools). straining to have a bowel movement and abdominal swelling or feeling of continued fullness after passing stools. Pay close attention to these symptoms and asks of yourself questions that may help in providing answers. This may save you a few bucks.

Gastroenteritis is inflammation (and our bodies are full of it) of the lining of the stomach intestines. You may have an intestinal virus, food poisoning, or you may have been drinking contaminated water or had too much alcohol.

The signs for gastroenteritis are: abdominal pains or cramping, nausea and/or vomiting, diarrhea, fever and/or chills. You must determine if you have an intestinal virus or food poisoning. A sign of food poisoning is if the people who ate with you have the same kind of sickness.

Lactose Intolerance: These conditions results from a lack of enzymes needed to digest sugar in dairy products.

Signs for lactose intolerance: abdominal cramping, pain and bloating after drinking milk or eating dairy products and having gas and diarrhea.

Menstrual Cramps: hormones changes which cause the uterus to go into spasms, and premenstrual bloating which increases abdominal pain.

Signs of menstrual cramps: mild to severe abdominal pain, back pain, fatigue and/or diarrhea and in some cases heavy bleeding or large blood clots. This is good information to share with your daughters so they can be on the lookout for future problems. Even with this symptom enzymes may help.

Peptic Ulcer: An ulcer in the stomach or small intestines. This can he brought on by stress, anger and holding on to past hurts.

Signs of a peptic ulcer: A gnawing or burning pain between the breastbone and the navel. This pain usually occurs between meals and in the mornings. The pain may last for a few minutes to a few hours. Taking antacids may relieve peptic ulcers temporary. This condition may be accompanied by the loss of appetite and weight loss, and nausea. (If you are losing weight rapidly without trying finding out why there may be a hidden health factor lurking in the wind). There may be vomiting of dark red blood, of something that looks like coffee grounds. There may also be bloody, black or tarry stools. Pay attention to your stool. Look for blood and any other thing that may be unusual and report to your doctor anything out of the ordinary.

Two (2) of the most common facts associated with peptic ulcers are:

1.  An infection with Helicobacter Pylon (usually called H. Pylon) bacteria.

2. The overuse of aspirin, and over the counter prescribed Ibuprofen.

Stomach Cancer: Most stomach cancer and stomach polyps are always linked to high fat and a low fiber diets. The older you get the higher the risk because of low stomach acid production and eating a diet containing less dietary fiber. You may also be an anemic. Smoking has a high risk factor and your dietary habits may contribute to an onset of a high intake of red meats and nitrates. Heavy use of alcohol and a low intake of fresh fruits and vegetables with vitamins C and E in them may inhabit the formation of nitrosamines. The gastric pathogen H. Pylori is strongly linked to stomach cancer, which is another result of nitrite metabolism.

In my case, H. Pylori was discovered by having a colonoscopy. I could not get rid of abdominal pains. So I search everywhere and that's when I found a cure for me it is called Siberian Pine Nut Oil. Shortly after taking Siberian Pine Nut Oil all of my symptoms went away. I had pains for months leading up to my discovery. I now keep Pine Nut Oil always in my home and will continue to keep it in my possession. It really works!

Signs of Stomach Cancer: Stomach pains after taking large amounts of antacids regularly, chronic indigestion, and heartburn or gas related reflux disease and gastritis, these all contribute to stomach cancer. Knowing the difference between acid reflux and stomach pain can make a big difference in how your doctors treat you.

Acid Reflux may be a constant burning in the upper chest and neck after eating which can cause burning, chests pains and even arm and back pains. Be aware of acid reflux and pay attention to what your body is experiencing. It may be easier to treat if you know what you are dealing with. It may save you a lot of money because you know the difference between acid reflux and a heart attack.

Colon Cancer: A cancer found in the colon or lower bowel which may be due to eating foods low in fiber. The major cause of this type of cancer is the ingestion of too much fat, red meat and refined carbohydrates which is the human body's key source of energy. If you are overweight and a smoker your risk is higher. Colon cancer may take years to develop and usually colitis and diabetics are common factors involved. Colon cancer has been moving up to become the second cause of death in our nation and at least 50,000 people die every year from it.

Signs of Colon Cancer Are: A persistent diarrhea that changes to a persistent constipation for no apparent reason. If you are seeing any blood in your bowel movements, it may change its appearance in the stool. Pay attention, blood in the stool becomes a thin flattened appearing mass. Often there is pain and gas in the lower right abdomen, unusual weight lost, and chronic fatigue (always asks why am I so tired. Your body may be trying to tell you something). Colon cancer begins as polyps found protruding from the inner wall of the colon.

Treatment for Colon Cancer: (Chemotherapy must be carefully considered by you, your doctor and family members).

Colon cancer depends on knowing the cause and by knowing the difference between major and minor stomach problems may hold your answer such as a mild stomachache or a severe stomach ache. Pains that persist can be a sign of a serious medical condition or illness. A very severe abdominal pain requires immediate medical attention. If you are taking chemotherapy and having abdominal pains there is a website call Chemocare.com which will help and give you many ways to help you take care of yourself during your chemotherapy treatments.

*Here I Stand:*

I am a cancer patient, a survivor, who did not take any chemotherapy in spite of the advice given to me by my health care providers. I personally don't feel comfortable giving advice or recommendations that I would not use for myself or my family. The advice in this book is what I personally learned for myself over the past 21 years.

I have tried to share with others what I have learned from living with and being a cancer patient myself. In this work, I have tried to share with others what I've learned as a cancer patient with two bouts with cancer. I have personally tried all of the information that I have shared with you and after 14 ½ years of survival, I am still alive and have a good quality of life. If it is the Lord's will, I still have the hope to be alive many years to come.

It is my opinion that before we can get started in exploring the healing process, we must first prepare ourselves to be healed. All healing no matter what the disease, in my opinion, happens when the sick person gets involved both physically and mentally to prepare to get healthy. Getting heal from cancer must start with the renewing of the mind. It begins by changing our attitude and our thinking about the way we look at healing. Also, having a healthy view of God and making note of what He has given us. In His creation, he has given our bodies an essential survival kit built inside of us. God gave us a soul with will and emotions. God made within our bodies a natural ability to heal itself. Our job is to study our bodies and to know what can help keep it healthy.

Therefore, I believe that upon diagnoses of cancer and before taking any medications or natural herbs, the first thing one must do is to examine oneself. You must consciously look at your life, lifestyle, and thinking. You must know yourself! How? By taking an in-depth look at what got you to this point in your life where sickness and disease have invaded you and taken over your body. So what happen?

The way to begin as I see it is by praying, asking God to search your heart and mind and to help you get rid of anything that will hinder you form being healed. Sadness and depression can block the healing process; therefore make your heart merry. Sing songs such as uplifting praise songs that will lift your spirit, warm your heart, and soothe the pain that is wracking your body. You must get rid of anything that will hinder you from your healing process, things like pinned up anger, malice, bitterness, grudges, jealousies, unforgiveness and etc. Instead of caring this big bag of rocks try practicing the fruit of the spirit which is love, peace, patience and gentleness, kindness and reverence etc.

A good antidote that will help you to get well is to rid yourself of anything that will hinder you from getting healed. Being unforgiving, and caring bitterness from your past can hinder you from getting healed and experiencing the greatness of God's presence in your life. Drop your giant bag of rocks that has been weighing you down for years. Let them go!

When I was at my worse, I remember being in so much pain until I didn't know what to do or how to pray. So I started singing, I sang a praise song called, "Halleluiah to the Lamb", I song with every fiber within my body, I song with praises in my heart and heaven on my mind. I song until the pain I was having started to actually leaving my body. I don't know how this happen but what I do know that from that day forward, I started to get better. As I felt better, I got busy with my research. When your heart is clean and your mind is clear and pure, then you can move mountains! And that's where I stand until this day standing on the mountain singing praise songs as loud as my lungs will let me. How good it is to sing praise songs to our God.

### *Some Of My Personal Dietary Remedies:*

This particular remedy was one of my first trials. I had been studying the benefits of garlic, onions and vinegar. So I came up with this bright idea that if I mixed the three and used them daily I might get some results and I did. Here's what I mixed and how I use it.

Make a mixture of garlic, onions and vinegar.

Chop some fresh garlic and place in a glass jar.

Chop up some fresh onions and place them in the same glass jar.

Mix in apple cider vinegar and fill the jar to the brim.

Keep the chopped mixture in the refrigerator:

(The mixture may turn green but it's ok as long as refrigerated)

Now, for the next two weeks put the mixture of onions, garlic and vinegar on all vegetables and soups that you eat. The smell of garlic will get into your skin and you will be able to smell the garlic in your skin. The garlic will act similar to chemotherapy and kill free radicals and parasite in your body and help the cells to rebuild themselves. To keep your breath fresh during this time use Breath Assured-a commonly used breath mint. You may also use parsley.

My next step was to detoxify my system. In my search I found a tea called Flora Essence Tea. This tea was used by the American Indians for various diseases and also much later used by President John F. Kennedy's family. A nurse named Marie Cassis later patented the tea. I take this tea every morning on an empty stomach.

I mix about 1 ounce of tea in a coffee cup filled with warm water, so I can sip it slowly.

I wait one hour before eating anything.

(Eating anything before the hour passes will make you sick)

With this tea and the mixture of garlic, onion and vinegar, I started noticing that I was feeling better. I had more energy. To this day I still drink this tea as a precautionary measure to maintain my health.

I also take Norwegian Cod Liver Oil daily. This helps to rebuild my Immune system and keeps my system healthy.

I take Flax Seed Oil, which is essentially Omega 3 oil. It helps keep my cholesterol down, my joints working properly and gives me overall energy.

I take Evening Primrose Oil and Vitamin E together. They help me with my breast. This combination may remove the lumps, that is not cancerous.

I also take Fish Oil and Siberian Pine Nut Oil.

I take a mixture of Barlean's Green in juice. The mixture rebuilds the immune system. If you have a family member who is taking Chemo, they need this product so they survive and minimize the side effects of chemotherapy.

I take Ultimate Flora Critical Care (Pro-biotic)

I also take multi-vitamins.

These are just a few of the natural products I took during and after my bouts with cancer. This just a few, but they will get your started in rebuilding your immune system.

Remember to always ask God to direct your path and lead you in the right directions to find your healing. Remember, God only heals those He wills. We cannot make demands on God but we can ask! You must also be resolving to accept His will. His will may not be to heal you or to extend your life, only God knows what He is going to do on your behalf. However, you can ask and keeping on asking until He reveals to you His plan for your life.

*A Few More Natural Helpful Hints I Have Used:*

**Ultimate Flora Critical Care:**

Is a pro-biotic formula rich in good bacteria. It can influence the makeup of your gut flora dramatically improving you overall health and well-being. A pro-biotic formula helps control problems with yeast in the colon area. All people have yeast lurking around their colon. It causes bloating and gas and can be annoying.

**Siberian Pine Nut Oil:**

It helps get rid of most stomach problems instantly. It helps with most gastrointestinal problems that include Helicobacter Pylori Infections. H. Pylori are a bacterial infection in the stomach or duodenum. H. Pylon secrete an enzyme that neutralized internal body acids. This acid enables the bacteria in the organs to survive and burrow into the coating in the lining of the stomach and duodenum that becomes irritated and inflamed. Small spirals like sores or ulcers develop. To help, take two tablespoons of Siberian Pine Nut Oil daily.

**Ginger:**

Ginger works with the digestive problems and aids in upset stomach, menstruation problems, vomiting etc.

**Turmeric:**

Turmeric is an anti-cancer fighting herb and can be used daily. It also helps with inflammation in the body.

**Sauerkraut:**

Sauerkraut is one of the number one sources in fighting cancer.

## Cinnamon:

Cinnamon helps in balancing the blood sugar for those who have diabetes. However, do not take cinnamon when the blood sugar is low. (I only take it when I have gone crazy on too many carbohydrates in one meal).

*Fight cancer in the digestive track and improve the immune system:*

This is one of the recipes I use to rebuild my immune system, improve my metabolism and help my digestive track stay healthy. I eat this recipe diet everyday and serve it to my family. I did not create this recipe but I found it in one of my studies from a book called "The Answer to Cancer" by Han Sharma, MD, Rama K. Mishra, G.A.M.S and James G. Meade, PH.D.

## Stewed Apple Recipe

Peel an apple (red or yellow delicious apple)

Cut it into 4 quarters and remove the core

Pierce the apple with 4 cloves, (I use 4 cloves per quarter)

Boil the combination in water for about 5 minutes to a nice softness.

Once the apple is cooked the way you like it, take out the cloves and throw them away. Don't eat them. Sip a nice cup of warm water along with it. Purified water is best.

Note: When you eat a cold apple, it just sits in your stomach. Do not use this recipe at night, because it builds up your metabolism. It should not be used to interfere with your sleep.

Note: I also watch the seasons and eat the fruits and vegetables of that season. For example, cherries clean the arteries. Pumpkins are high in antioxidants and build the immune system for that month. Try boiling them and eating them other than a pumpkin pie. They are good and good for you. By the way look for foods in season and try to develop a taste for the foods of the earth. God created them for a purpose and that purpose was to save our lives. Learn to love them and appreciate them because they may be the key to getting your body healthy again.

### *My Personal Formula for Getting Healthy:*

Flora Essence Tea

Barlean's Greens

Flax Seed Oil or Mixed Flour

Fish Oil

Evening Primrose Oil

Vitamins C, E, A

Vitamin D 3

Enzymes

Butcher Broom

Yellow Dock

Horse Chestnut Extract or Venastat (for poor circulation)

Cinnamon for lowering blood sugar)

Red Clover (to shrink tumors)

CANCER: A SENTENCE TO LIVE

Included is the Stewart Apple Diet (which aids digestion and stomach balance). Also included is the onion, garlic and apple cider vinegar and all vegetables.

These are just a few of what I personally used, however, when you start on your own personal research you to will discover your own personal helps. As you discover what works best for you share with others. We may just wipe out cancer one person at a time.

## *The Benefits of Red Clover*

Comes In Tea or Tablets

Red Clover reduces hot flashes.

Slows down bone lost

Helps with menopause.

Raises bone density.

Reduce the risk of heart disease.

Increased the amount of good cholesterol.

Improves the quality of arteries so blood can flow more efficiently through the system.

Red clover slows down and prevents the spread of cancer cells-before they can affect other parts of the body.

Red clover can relieve symptoms of eczema, psoriasis and skin rashes.

Red clover can be used for a decongestion and cough medicine

Red clover can be used for cold sores and sore throat (gargle & swish).

Red clover helps improve circulation.

Red clover carries many natural vitamins and nutrients, magnesium potassium, and niacin.

Red clover promotes healthy bloom steam.

### *Do you know the warning signs of a Stroke?*

Knowing the warning signs of a stroke and getting proper medical attention and treatment could mean the difference between life and death and permanent disability.

Classic Stroke Symptoms:

Sudden numbness, weakness, a paralysis of face, arm or leg usually on one side of your body.

Sudden difficulty speaking or understanding speech.

Sudden blurred, double or decreased vision.

Sudden dizziness, loss of balance or coordination.

A sudden severe headache or unusual headache, which may be accompanied by a stiff neck, facial pain, pain between your eyes, vomiting or altered unconsciousness.

Confusion or problems with memory, spatial orientation or perception.

These warning signs can save your life. Place them where you and your family members can watch for any symptoms in each other. Pay attention! Strokes are dangerous and when you visit the nursing homes, you see the evidence of a stroke in the old and young.

*Five Helpful Hints to treat arthritis naturally:*

Exercise

Diet

Cold and hot therapy

Acupuncture

Glucosamine and Chondroirin

ER Pain Relief

Foot Source Machine

The Rife Machine

# RESOURCES

*Internet Resources:*
Bottom Line Secrets (bottomlinesecrets@bls.bottomlinesecrets.com )
Harvard Medical School (Healthbeat@hms.harvard.edu )
Dr. Alan Inglis and Dr. Douglas (recs@realadvantagesvitimins.com )
Daily Health News (dailyhealthnew@dhn.bottomlinesecrets.com )
Health Talk (health@healthtalk.com )
North Star Team (nsne@northstarvitimins.com )
HIS-Jenny Thompson (hsirresearch@healtheirnews.com )
Nutrition and Healing-Amanda Ross (healthtips@healltheirnews.com )
WC Douglas (Realhealth@realhealthnews.com )
Digestive Health Smart Brief (dnsb@smartbrief.com )
Cancer Defeated (custserv@cancerdefeated.com )

*Hospitals and Clinics Recommend:*
The Mayo Clinic
Jacksonville, Florida

Johns Hopkins Hospital
Baltimore, Maryland

The Medical Center Of Central Georgia
Macon, Georgia
The Coliseum Hospitals
Macon, Georgia

Nutritional Consultants
Dr. James Denny
Macon, Georgia

*Book Resources:*
The Complete Guide to Herbal Medicines by:
Charles W. Ferrow, PharmiD.
Juan R. Avila, Pharmifl.

Bottom Line Secret Food Cures & Doctor-Approved Folk Remedies
By: Joan When and Lydia Wilen
Beating Cancer with Nutrition by: Patrick Quillin, PHD. RO .CNS
With Noreen Quillin

Whole Body Massage by: Nitya Lacroix,
Francesca Rinaldi, Sharon Seager, Renee Tanner

Healthy Healing 121 Edition
By: Linda Page Ph.D.

Stopping Cancer at the Source
By: M. Sara Rosenthal, Ph.D.

Healing Herbs
The Essential Guide
By: H Winter Griffith, M.D.

A History of Medicine
Second Edition

By: Lois N. Magner
Bible Study Methods
Rick Warren

Cancer Fighting Machines: I use for my cancer treatments:
The Rife Machine
The Rife Machine Wellness Technology
For Diabetics-Cancer-Pain-Chronic Fatigue-Lyme-fibromyalgia-Impotence
and Infertility. . ..550 Conditions and More

The Rebuilding Model 2407
Rebuilder Medical Technology, Inc.

The foot Choice Model #YS-322
Combines the top-3 Pain Relieving Technologist in 1 Therapeutic Device
Infrared Heat, Reflexology and Message Therapy

The Smarty Sauna
The Whole Body Hypothermia Treatment System
A Detoxifying Machine

Take a bit of will power, the ability to study and acquire knowledge, add a healthy bit of skepticism and above all, add great faith in the healing power of a strong belief in God. Couple this with an unquenchable sense of joy and then have a picture of a dynamic resourceful woman who, by learned accounts, should not be still here on earth. Evelyn Pettie Reid should be dead. She should not have survived for eight years beyond the period set for her by cancer physicians in several southeastern states, but she did. Now, she has a strong, very strong desire to share her battle with cancer with anyone who will listen. It's her mission. She wants to help others, family and friends, learn how they too can learn to deal with the effects of cancer in their lives as well.

I believe this book is evidence that Evelyn Pettie Reid has found a powerful way to get her message of the power of faith, knowledge and hope out to the world. Perhaps you, her readers, will join her and spread the word.

*George Foster*

# ABOUT THE AUTHOR

# EVELYN MAXINE PETTIE REID

Evelyn was born in Martinsville, Virginia. She is the daughter of the Late Dana B. and Martha R. Pettie. She is one of eleven children. She was educated in the Martinsville and Henry County Public School Systems. She is a graduate of George Washington Carver High School and Kittrell Jr. College. in North Carolina. She attended Howard University, majoring in Mass Communications and Print Media; she graduated from Barbizon Modeling School of Atlanta and Frankie Shelton's School of Floral Designs in Memphis, Tennessee. She is a 1993 Graduate of Crossroads Institute of Biblical Studies and she is currently studying Natural Homeopathy Medicine at Clayton College.

Evelyn is the founder of Image Alive Modeling School and Agency and Beauty of The Earth Floral Designs, Fashions and Publishing Co. She also founded, I Can Fashions and RoNees Fashion Floor. She is a writer and recording artist. She has written and recorded songs such as Husband, The Morning Song, My Desire, and Teach Me to Number My Days, Your Will Lord and The Place Where Your Glory Dwells. She has been an Actress and Play Writer; she has starred in the traveling play by Beverly Banks Miller, called True Love.

Her background also includes radio and television: WHMM-TV32 Washington, D.C., WYCB Radio, Washington, D.C. KLUM-FM Lincoln University, in Jefferson City, Missouri. She has performed as the Midnight Star on WIBB, WDDO and WFNE Radio Macon, GA and a radio talk show hostess for the program ISSUES OF LIFE on WBML Christian Radio Macon, Georgia.

Currently, Evelyn is the professor of Women's Studies at Crossroads Institute of Biblical Studies.

Evelyn is married to Rev., Dr. Donald M. Reid, pastor and founder of the Aletheia Baptist Church and Founder and President of Crossroads Institute of Biblical Studies in Macon, Georgia. She is the mother of one daughter, Leni Shontae Wilson, who is a graduate of Hampton University. God has blessed Evelyn and Donald with a grand son Evan Donald Simmons who brings much joy and completed happiness. She had two godchildren Ni'eema Johnson and McKenzie Grace Seay.

CPSIA information can be obtained
at www.ICGtesting.com
Printed in the USA
LVHW030338260219
608762LV00003B/350/P